RadiantBOOKS
Gospel Publishing House/Springfield. Mo 65802

02-0881

© 1982 by the Gospel Publishing House, Springfield, Missouri 65802. All rights reserved. No part of this book may be reproduced, stored in a retrieval system, or transmitted in any form or by any means, electronic, mechanical, photocopy, recording, or otherwise, without prior written permission of the copyright owner, except brief quotations used in connection with reviews in magazines or newspapers.

Library of Congress Catalog Card Number 81-84763
International Standard Book Number 0-88243-881-6
Printed in the United States of America

A teacher's guide for individual or group study with this book is available from the Gospel Publishing House.

Contents

1

It's Your Decision

Deciding to Decide

Whether you remain single for a lifetime or marry after a period of singleness is for you alone to decide. This decision is too important to be left to others; be they parents, peers, or anyone else. You alone must decide.

Some young people have the idea that fate will make the decision for them, that their destiny is hidden in the stars. Others feel that there is only one person in the world they can marry and be in God's will. As a loving Father, God is very interested in whom you marry and is concerned with your marital happiness. However, His Word does not support the assumption that He will pick a mate for you. And life is not a game in which you must find the secret that God has so cleverly hidden. He loves His children too much to play games with their happiness.

Learning to make decisions is an art that comes only through personal experience. In childhood most of our decisions were made for us. In adolescence we attempted more independence in decisionmaking. To the degree that we made good decisions, we have confidence in our powers of choice. To the degree that we made bad decisions, we fear making further choices. Fear of making choices (*decidophobia)* is said to be the most prevalent emotional illness among young people today.

Romantic choices have such long-term consequences that they must be made carefully and prayerfully. We must combine sound principles of decisionmaking with spiritual insights if we are to have confidence in our powers of choice.

Decisionmaking is the process by which a person chooses from two or more alternatives or possible solutions. Decisionmaking differs from problem solving in that decisions are made from opportunities of equal value. Problem solving, on the other hand, involves selecting the best solution from a number of unequal options.

Choosing a mate is not solving a problem. It is not the process of looking for the best among several unequal solutions. Selecting a partner for Christian marriage is usually a process of choosing from several eligible options, any one of which could be an acceptable choice. This is especially true when dating is restricted to Christians who are striving to be led by the Holy Spirit. And, the opportunity to remain single is a viable option in the romantic decisionmaking process.

Becoming Decisive

You become a decisive person as you make and evaluate your choices. The decisive person has more personal freedom than others simply because he is able to recognize, discover, and create new opportunities for decisionmaking.

The decisive person also has more control over

his personal life because he can reduce the amount of uncertainty in his choices and is able to limit the degree to which chance influences his future. Joshua pointed this out to the nation of Israel when he called them to choose God rather than paganism (Joshua 24:15). He openly recognized that his decisions influenced not only himself, but also his household. Romantic decisions always influence a widening circle of other people who will be either included or excluded by the final choice.

Becoming decisive demands that we become responsible for our own behavior and refuse to blame others for circumstances that may influence our decisions. It also forces us to face the fact that we are responsible only for the decision—we have little control over the outcome. How others respond to our decision is part of their free moral agency. Otherwise, their response is not a product of free choice, but is the result of manipulation.

In decisionmaking, we must come to terms with time and recognize that much of romantic interacting is a matter of being at the right place at the right time. When we have made a decision, however, we end our deliberations. To make a decision and then go back and do a postmortem on it is to fail to be decisive.

Limit on Decisionmaking

Freedom in decisionmaking is seldom unlimited. The wise Christian looks at the limitations on his decisionmaking powers and works constructively within those limits.

1. *Capability*. What a person is capable of

doing is represented by his capacities and abilities. How well he functions is limited by the capacity God has given him physically and mentally, and how well he has developed the ability to accomplish the tasks of life. Energy levels, I.Q., complexion, height, genetic abnormalities, and results of accidents or disease that are obvious in dating will continue to be present in marriage (2 Samuel 4:4; 9:12,13; Jeremiah 13:23; Luke 12:25).

2. *Interest.* What a person does is a reflection of his motivation. It is an indication of what his values are. To decide to marry a person with the intention of changing him is a violation of his God-given dignity. The compulsion to change another individual is not rooted in love, but selfishness.

When there are differences in goals and value systems, each person must take an honest look at his own motivations. Each must assess the strengths of the values that are at variance. If the discrepancy is too great, a reevaluation of the relationship is warranted (Acts 15:37-40; 2 Timothy 4:11). To refuse to be honest about expectations is to delay inevitable heartache.

3. *Place.* Decisions are always influenced by opportunities. It is true that the Lord has a marvelous way of bringing the paths of His children to cross, but we must not leave to the caprice of chance the meeting of individuals who could add a meaningful dimension to our lives. A simple cliché may be helpful: Christians should hang out where Christians gather. The opportunities of meeting interesting friends of both sexes are enlarged when we develop interests in hobbies,

8

recreation, and spiritual activities that attract Christians.

4. *Time.* Timing is important in relationships. Being in the right place at the right time works wonders. This points out the importance of keeping appointments, meeting deadlines, and avoiding procrastination. The way a person handles time is a strong indication of what he thinks of himself and the respect he has for others.

5. *Data.* Making decisions before adequate data have been collected is disastrous. It is essential to get all the information available before reaching a conclusion and initiating action.

6. *Experience.* There is no substitute for experience in decisionmaking. Current decisions are influenced by previous ones. Legal, ethical, and societal decisions of others also influence our own decisions. We owe it to ourselves to be knowledgeable in decisionmaking.

7. *Lack of alternatives.* One of the fallacies in making romantic decisions is to assume that no alternatives are available. The result is to make a premature choice. Dates who appear so charming in the teen years may well lose their appeal in a few years as more mature alternatives emerge and our perceptions change. Divorce courts echo with the testimonies of young people who made a premature commitment only to plead to be released so they can make another marital choice.

Requirements for Decisionmaking

There are basically three requirements in the process of good decisionmaking as it relates to romantic choices: values, information, and strategy.

1. *Values.* Values are those things we hold dear; they become the guiding principles of life. They are an outgrowth of beliefs, preferences, and attitudes that we have spent a lifetime developing. Values are the foundation and integrating framework for the decisionmaking process. They determine what will be satisfying for us and help us set our objectives. Values also dictate what action should be taken to reach our objectives.

All values are learned. They are the result of study and experience. When we incorporate the values of the kingdom of heaven (Matthew 5 to 7) into our daily lives, our choices and actions become consistent with Scripture (2 Timothy 2:15; 3:16,17).

The kinds of decisions made in dating and the attitudes displayed while waiting for marriage are a reflection of a person's values.

2. *Information.* The knowledge we have gained through study and experience influences the decisions we make. It is at this point that prayer and Bible study are so important in ascertaining the will of God (Jeremiah 33:3; Romans 10:17; Philippians 4:4-8). In connection with this, Wayne Oates says: "Faith becomes the main ingredient in risky decisionmaking, generously mixed with what little data we can gather in the time we have" (Wayne E. Oates, *The Psychology of Religion* [Waco, TX: Word Books, Inc., 1973], p. 202).

3. *Strategy.* Strategy is the way to convert values and information into action. Strategy helps us estimate the risk involved in each alter-

native, as we tie together personal values and information with our objectives.

Some choices are 100 percent certain—such as the odds of getting wet if you jump into a river with your clothes on. Other strategies involve risks of varying degrees of certainty.

There are also strategies with unknown probabilities. Most decisions involve a combination of risk and uncertainty. Here are some guidelines to use in developing a strategy for making romantic choices:

a. *Know your personal values.* Be honest about what is important to you now and will continue to be important to you in the future.

b. *State your objectives clearly.* This includes what you have to offer in marriage as well as what you expect to get out of marriage.

c. *Rank your goals.* In descending order of importance, rank your goals in life and estimate your chance of attaining each one. What alternatives do you have if you are blocked from attaining any of your higher order goals? The spiritual dimensions of your goals are extremely important at this point.

Process of Decisionmaking

Making good decisions is a process. We will look at the pattern and then apply it to dating and waiting.

1. Define the decision to be made.

2. Know what is important to you and why you want to accomplish this goal.

3. Examine the information you already have about your alternatives.

4. Seek new information related to your goals.

11

5. Assess the risks and costs involved in each alternative open to you.

6. Develop a plan of action.

7. Make the decision.

Now let's look at the process from a romantic point of view:

1. *Decision to be made.* Shall I remain single or get married? Could I best serve the Lord as a single or in marriage?

2. *Goals to be achieved.* Make a list of what you would like to accomplish in life. Establish specific goals for 5 years, 10 years, and 25 years from now.

3. *Examination of information.* How many of these goals are possible as a single? Make a list. How many require marriage? Make a list.

4. *Information search.* What additional information do you need to assist you in making a valid decision? Where can you secure the needed information, guidance, or counsel?

5. *Assessment of risks.* How would being single assist or interfere with any of your goals? What goals would marriage delay? What goals would marriage hamper or eliminate?

6. *Plan of action.* Glean from your list what you consider the core values you must achieve to be a fulfilled person. Put an asterisk in front of those things that should be accomplished before marriage. Are you willing to delay marriage to achieve those goals? If not, are those goals really that important to you? What strain would it put on the marriage if you tried to reach those goals as a married person? What pressures would it put on a spouse or children if you tried to reach those goals after you started your family?

7. *Decision to be implemented.* What should

you do? Remain single? Plan for marriage? Is it a two-step decision that requires more time as a single before entering marriage?

Hopefully, by this time, you have come to see that the decision to marry or remain single is not something to be determined while huddled in romantic seclusion. This decision is far too important to allow it to be influenced by chemistry or the moon's reflection on a romantic river.

This approach to decisionmaking will not select the right person for you, but it will give you information about yourself that you need before you get your priorities straight and decide what the most important things in your life are.

As a final exercise, explore your romantic potential by responding to the following items adapted from *A Guidebook to Dating, Waiting, and Choosing a Mate*, by H. Norman Wright and Marvin Inmon (Irvine, CA: Harvest House Publishers, 1973; pp. 5-7):

1. List five healthy reasons for remaining single.

2. List five unhealthy reasons for remaining single.

3. List five healthy reasons for getting married.

4. List five unhealthy reasons for getting married.

5. List some possible benefits of remaining single.

6. List some possible limitations of married life.

7. List some possible benefits of married life.

8. List some possible limitations of remaining single.

Now, broaden the focus of your attention to cover the entire scope of life.

2
Three Big Decisions

Establishing Priorities

If you are to live life to the fullest as Christ wants you to, there are three big decisions you must make. Ironically, these decisions are usually made in the first third of life, but they strongly influence the remainder of life. The order in which these decisions are made is extremely crucial.

The most important decision of a lifetime is to choose Christ as your Lord and Master. This decision handles your past, prepares you for the future, and gives you assurance for today. When the other important decisions of life are made within the privileges and responsibilities of the kingdom of heaven, successful living is assured.

The second major decision you must make is your career choice. What you are going to do in life as a career will not only affect your happiness but also establish the atmosphere in which you will live. Your career choice needs to be made before a romantic choice is finalized, because your choice of career will tremendously influence where you will live and under what conditions.

The third most important decision you will make is whether or not you will marry and, if so,

14

who and when. The reasons why the choice of a companion should follow the career choice will emerge as we look at the influence the career has on marital happiness.

When the marital choice is made before a person's Christian commitment is complete, the marriage relationship becomes unequal (2 Corinthians 6:14). The one coming to Christ is frequently hampered from making a total commitment to Christ by the spouse who is not responsive to spiritual goals and values (1 Peter 3:1-7).

When the marital choice is made before the career choice, the future is more uncertain than necessary. The kind of person who would be happy married to a mate in one type of career might very well be uncomfortable with a spouse in another profession. For instance, the girl who would be happy as the wife of a doctor or lawyer might be miserable as the wife of a plumber or carpenter. It is not that one type of career is superior to another, but that the demands on the home and family are very different with different types of careers. The socioeconomic level on which the couple lives and the kinds of friends and activities they enjoy will also vary with the type of career chosen. This is not a popular position with young people, but these conclusions emerge from studies of couples with various levels of education and their reported happiness.

It sounds glamorous to meet in college, fall in love, marry, and put "hubby" through to his degree. But, the fact of the matter is that an unusually high number of college romances do not survive because of the added pressures that schooling puts on the traditional demands of work and adjustment to marriage.

First Things First

The most important decision of life is establishing your relationship with God. John 3:16 tells of God's love for us. Paul tells of our universal need for God (Romans 3:23; 6:23). He also tells us how to come to God (Romans 10:9,10). When we accept Christ as the Son of God and invite Him to become our Lord and Master, He introduces a new set of principles into our lives that give us the guidelines for successful Christian living.

No decision is more important. Turning to God as our Father brings forgiveness for sin. Guilt, which plagued our lives because of our knowledge that we had sinned against a holy God, is removed. When we ask Christ to come into our lives and to forgive us of our sins, He performs a miracle of regeneration. Our sins are forgiven. They are covered by the blood of Jesus Christ (1 John 1:7); they are separated from us as far as the east is from the west, never to be remembered against us anymore (Psalm 103:12). This is complete forgiveness!

One powerful force in the universe is fear. When Christ comes into our lives, He removes the taint of sin. Nothing from our past is left for us to fear. It is completely wiped out! We also recognize that our future is in the hands of Christ. That leaves nothing lurking ahead for us to worry about.

Since Christ has the future in His hands and our past has been forgiven, the only concern left is for the unanticipated emergencies that arise in everyday living. Here is where the Holy Spirit comes in, for His purpose in our lives as believers is to lead us and guide us into all truth (John 16:13).

As we study God's Word and are led by the Holy Spirit, we receive divine insights. These insights are part of the information we need to make good decisions. The Holy Spirit not only reveals sins, but also points out the "weights" that could cling to our lives and interfere with our Christian testimony (Hebrews 12:1). Here is where we really order our priorities and put into proper perspective those things that may not be sin but are unnecessary in our lives (1 Corinthians 6:12).

Knowing the "thou shalts" and the "thou shalt nots" of Scripture gives us guidelines for making our decisions. We must be aware not only of the potential of sins of commission, but also of the sins of omission. Living by divine principles sets the parameters of life for us and gives us the latitude we need for effective Christian living. When we do make mistakes, we know we have an Advocate with the Father who is interceding for us (Romans 8:1; 2 Corinthians 5:17; 1 John 1:9; 2:1).

Choosing a Career

Choosing a career is a very personal matter. No two individuals are the same, so there are no simple formulas for all to follow in making this strategic choice. Choosing a career is a function of personality development. Different types of personalities are more adept at one type of career than another. And, varieties of personality types are represented in each career.

17

There are 21,741 separate occupations defined under 35,550 different titles in the 1965 edition of the *Dictionary of Occupational Titles* (Washington, D.C.: U.S. Government Printing Office; Vol. 1, p. xv). And, new jobs are being created every day. It is estimated that more than half of the jobs that will be available to young workers at the turn of the century have not even been invented yet.

Task number one in choosing a career is to discover who you are and get a grip on the real you. Here are some preliminary things you need to know about yourself in career exploration:

1. *Abilities.* What abilities do you have? These represent your *powers to do,* the things you have learned to perform. Are there dormant abilities that you have not yet developed? You may need to practice more, exercise more, or study more. But, to develop your potential is essential if you are to have a wide scope of options in your career exploration.

2. *Interests.* What do you enjoy doing? Interests represent your *will to do.* Are your interests so varied that you enjoy doing more things than you can get around to? Are they so narrow that nothing excites you? Flexibility needs to be developed here, because you must enjoy the majority of tasks related to your job or you will be disillusioned with it.

One of the major problems of industry today is monotony. This form of boredom comes either from a lack of interest in what is going on or from a lack of ability to muster adequate motivation to stick to the job. Unfortunately, monotony is usually followed by apathy and that is a destructive attitude for career fulfillment.

3. *Opportunities.* Opportunity begins with your part-time job in high school and follows you through your entire work experience. The more varied the jobs you explore—even if you work as a volunteer without pay—the more data you can collect for making the right kind of career decisions.

On the other hand, to have the ability for and an interest in a job that is not available to you only guarantees unemployment. Many times you have to start with the job that is available, even if it is not the one you want. Entrance into the work force usually is on the ground level. Then your skills and concentration can be observed and lead to a promotion. You have to begin somewhere. There is much to be said for the virtues of honest work, even in an age when the work ethic is not popular (Ecclesiastes 9:10; Acts 18:3; Ephesians 6:5-10; Colossians 3:22-25). Slothfulness is never a Christian virtue (Proverbs 12:24,27).

Marks of Maturity

It takes a mature person to make a valid career choice. Two essentials of maturity have been isolated: (1) the ability to delay gratification, and (2) the ability to be responsible for your own behavior.

The capacity to delay gratification shows itself in the ability to make good plans. There are basically three kinds of plans to be made: immediate, intermediate, and ultimate. Planning for life involves long-range planning. This is what you were asked to do in the previous chapter; that is, to establish some goals for 5, 10, and 25 years from now.

It is necessary to have some ultimate goals as a guiding star to draw your attention and motivation to higher levels of achievement. When you have set your ultimate goals, specifically those that relate to career and family, you can then turn to your intermediate goals. What are the steps you must go through to reach your ultimate goals? What education is required? Is it college or vocational on-the-job training? When you have explored your intermediate goals, you can then turn to your immediate goals.

What do you need to be doing now to be eligible to enter the activities required by your intermediate goals? If you are still in high school, what kind of grades should you be making in order to be admitted to the college, vocational school, or industrial training program of your choice? If you are in college, what courses should you be taking to prepare yourself adequately for admission to a profession or vocation? What would be a good supporting study area? Should it be a minor or a second major? What kind of grade-point average is required?

One thing is clear: if you do not enjoy the process of becoming eligible for a career, the chances are good that you will not enjoy the career when you are in it. That is why it is important to keep broad options and seek a variety of work experiences.

With the uncertainty of the job market today, it is important to look at personality variables. Very few people lose a job because they do not know how to do it. Most firings in business and industry occur because of personality conflicts. Adaptability is the most important quality you can take with you into the job market.

It also must be acknowledged that most adults make three major job changes in their working years. These changes are usually within job families rather than major shifts, but it is not uncommon for a person to enter a job area, work his way up, and move on to a new area that utilizes some of the skills he already has and trains him to develop new ones. You don't have to allow yourself to be "pigeonholed" in a job you don't like. Work your way through to a new opportunity.

Being responsible for your own behavior is another dimension of maturity. It requires you to follow through on your decisions without shifting blame to others or rationalizing yourself out of responsibility. Decisiveness demands responsibility. This is basic to the maturity that marriage demands.

The Marital Choice

In a takeoff on Shakespeare, "To marry or not to marry, that is the question." Drawing on the lists suggested at the end of chapter 1, what healthy reasons did you come up with for remaining single? How do these compare with your healthy reasons for marriage? Did you conclude that marriage may be for you sometime, somewhere, but not now? If so, you fall in the category of perfectly "normal."

In subsequent chapters we will look at some of the essentials in making the marriage choice. It will be necessary to look at yourself, for it is more important for you to become the right person for marriage than to find the right one. Consideration must be given to becoming a total person in all the dimensions of what it means to be a normal Christian adult.

Consideration should also be given to the differences between the sexes as well as the potential for compatibility. It is in establishing the bases of compatibility before marriage that you can enter marriage with the assurance that it is to be for a lifetime.

In a discussion of "taking the risk out of mate selection," H. Norman Wright offers some suggestions concerning compatibility. He notes:

> The results of hundreds of studies of married couples indicate that, almost without exception, in physical, social, and psychological characteristics the mates were more alike than different. The exceptions, or those that appear to be exceptions, do not alter this overall tendency.
>
> Within the framework of like marrying like, however, some characteristics appear to be quite opposite in each spouse. Since the fulfillment of needs is at the heart of much of mate selection, one will find that some needs in couples are complementary while some are contradictory. (H. Norman Wright, *Premarital Counseling* [Chicago: Moody Press, 1977], pp. 24,25.)

Where there are complementary needs in the relationship, Wright observes, no compromise is necessary. But where the needs are contradictory, finding a middle ground is necessary. This compromise will not necessarily be a happy medium. Wright continues: "For example, if one is extremely thrifty and the other is a big spender, the needs will clash head-on. If one enjoys social contacts and the other is a recluse, conflict is almost inevitable."

The processes through which you collect adequate information for making the marital choice need to be examined. Mature decisions must be based on information and knowledge, not emotional stimulation. It is easy to be tempted to make marital choices under the stimulation of romantic experiences or expectations from peers. This leads to unhealthy attitudes and actions that bring guilt. The result is heartache for all concerned.

But, you are not left alone to make these decisions. By maintaining an active devotional life and sharing fellowship with a body of believers, you have the opportunity to experience the broad dimensions of emotions that accompany the decisionmaking process.

If you make these decisions in the proper order, you can be assured of success and happiness. If you have not already done so, choose Christ as Lord before you proceed further. Explore the world of work and select a career that suits your abilities and interests. Then, keep your options open for the kind of romantic involvements in life that may lead to a Christian marriage and family. This is just the beginning, however, for decisionmaking is a lifelong venture.

3
Becoming the Right Person

Who Are You?

Yes, it is more important to become the right person for a relationship than to find the right person to marry. But how do you discover who you are? Everyone, sometime in growing up, must stop and ask himself two basic questions: "Who am I?" and, "Why am I here?" These questions will determine the fullness with which you can explore life.

If you have made the first decision presented in the previous chapter and have chosen a personal relationship with God, you can respond to the first question positively. You are a child of God, born into His kingdom through the sacrifice of His Son, and declared to be an heir with Christ of all things that pertain to the kingdom of heaven (Romans 8:17).

When you know who you are, then you can approach the second question: "Why am I here?" Again the Bible has the answer.

The early chapters of Genesis tell us that God created man special. All creation had been brought into being by the voice of God, but man alone was formed by the hand of God, custommade, if you please. God breathed into man the breath of life, and man became a living soul (Genesis 1:26-28). Again, the woman was custom-made from the material taken from the side of man (Genesis 2:21,22). Creation, then, testifies to the uniqueness of mankind in the universe and to the special place we have in the plan of God.

Why Are You Here?

The Bible gives at least four reasons for the existence of us all:

1. *To love God.* The first reason for being born is given in Deuteronomy 6:4-6: to love God. When Jesus was asked what the most important commandment was, He quoted this passage from the writings of Moses (Mark 12:28-31). To the unspoken question: "How should we love God?" Jesus responded by saying with our heart, soul, mind, and strength. These four dimensions of being incorporate the total human personality: thinking, feeling, and doing.

Jesus was simply saying, "Love God with all of yourself." How do you show that you love Him? By keeping His commandment (John 14:15). What commandment? The commandment to love one another (John 13:34). Our love for God, then, is shown in the way we treat one another in everyday life.

2. *To reverence God.* Solomon gives us two reasons for being born and calls them "the whole duty of man" (Ecclesiastes 12:13). The first is to fear God. This means to reverence Him, to stand in awe of who He is as the Creator of the universe. David and Solomon both tell us that "the fear of the LORD is the beginning of wisdom" (Psalm 111:10; Proverbs 9:10).

Very simply, then, to know who we are and to become what we were created to become requires us to develop a relationship of reverence and respect for God.

3. *To obey God.* To reverential fear for God, Solomon adds obedience to His Word as a reason for our existence (Ecclesiastes 12:13). God has given us His Word to light our path and to guide us in life (Psalm 119:105). That is why it is so important to study the Bible (2 Timothy 2:15). It tells us what God wants us to do (Psalm 119:11).

4. *To worship God.* Another reason for the creation of mankind in general, and you in particular, is for the pleasure of God. This pleasure comes from the worship of the redeemed (Revelation 4:11).

Now that you know who you are and why you are here, the question is, do you like yourself? The view you have of yourself will affect all of your relationships with others. Your self-concept, the way you accept or reject yourself, is one of the most important factors in determining what kind of person you will become.

Becoming Yourself

Coming to grips with yourself as a total person may be difficult, but it is basic to becoming the right person for successful single living as well as for contributing to the welfare of another in Christian marriage. Here are some steps to guide you in discovering who you really are.

1. *Accept yourself.* Look in the mirror. Do you like what you see? If not, what can you do about it? Accepting yourself requires you to determine those things about you that you like, those that

you think need to be changed, and those that cannot be changed. Some things can be improved with exercise and self-discipline. Others must be accepted. But the secret is to change what you want to—and are capable of changing—and to accept that which God has given you to make you unique.

Accepting yourself involves liking yourself, feeling a quiet pleasure in being just who you are. This brings with it the emotional security of being able to like yourself as good company.

2. *Extend yourself.* Beyond accepting yourself, reach out and touch someone. Unless you develop strong interests outside yourself, you will become selfish and live on a less than human level. Your maturity will advance to the degree that your life is decentered from the clamorous immediacy of satisfying the demands of body and self. All of us need to reach out and share creatively with others, whether we are single or married.

3. *Relate warmly to others.* This involves responding to others in such a way that we experience a full affectional relationship. This is the kind of loving relationship that comes in the Christian community when we know what it means to be our brother's keeper and sense the empathy of the Good Samaritan (Luke 10:30-37). This feeling is best illustrated by the *agape* love that Jesus tells us to have for one another, the love that gives and expects nothing in return (1 John 4:7,8).

In a developing romantic relationship, this warmth of feeling allows you to respond lovingly to another person without becoming erotically involved.

4. *Open yourself to experience.* This is a free experiencing of all of your senses and sensations without analyzing what is happening to you. It is the cool breeze on your warm face, your hair flying in the wind, or the ache of muscles that have had a good workout. In relationships, this openness involves giving rather than being concerned about receiving. In marriage, this will broaden to accept the sensations of lovemaking with gratitude for the Creator who made male and female uniquely and wonderfully (Psalm 139:14).

Being open to new experiences allows you to enjoy new flavors, new sounds, and new aromas, and to explore the full emotional normalcy that comes with the peak experiences of raptness and ecstasy.

5. *Be objective about yourself.* Objectivity has two dimensions: insight and humor.

Insight involves coming to a good understanding of yourself. It brings into harmony the three dimensions of self: who you are as *God* knows you, who *others* think you are, and who *you* think you are. It is like focusing a camera. When you get the images in the viewfinder synchronized, the picture is ready to shoot. When you get the various perspectives of yourself together—God's, others', and yours—you are being real, genuine, transparent.

The other dimension of objectivity is humor. This is the attribute that allows you to laugh when you are sad, see light when it is dark, and find joy in living. It also allows you to see the ridiculous in life. Humor is an absolute essential in human relationships for both marrieds and singles.

So often we have a tendency to take life too seriously. It reminds me of a poster my father placed by my workbench in his shoe shop while I was growing up and he was teaching me the cobbler's trade. The message of the sign was simple: "Don't take life too seriously; you'll never get out of it alive anyhow!" Now that I am older I can appreciate what he was trying to tell me. He detected my tendency to be too serious and tried to warn me in his own unique way.

6. *Be reality oriented.* This requires us to be in close touch with the real world around us and not live in air castles or build barriers between ourselves and others. It involves developing the ability to love and create, to emerge from childlike ties to family, and to mature by finding out who we are as separate entities. This allows us to look outside ourselves as well as to be true to our inner selves. It allows us to develop objectivity and reason based on who we are in relationship to God and His universe.

Sober Thinking

Paul is concerned that we should think properly about ourselves. He cautions against high thinking that distorts reality (Romans 12:3). Although he does not mention low thinking, the fact that thinking too highly is given as an extension from sober thinking implies that it is just as possible to think too lowly as it is to think too highly. Low thinking was not the problem of the Roman church, but it is a very serious problem today.

The sequence is simple: thoughts lead to attitudes. Attitudes cannot be measured; they can only be inferred by behavior. So the thoughts that lead to attitudes are seen by the behavior of the thinker.

Thoughts	Attitudes	Behavior
High	Pride	Superior
Sober	Realistic	Balanced
Low	Depreciating	Inferior

An attitude is a predisposition to respond consistently with feeling to the opportunities of life, be they people, places, things, or ideas. Another word for predisposition is stance, which implies posture. Think of the stance of the baseball batter as it differs from that of the catcher, or the stance of the football center as it differs from that of the linebacker. Attitudes are mental positions that allow us to respond to appropriate signals.

The high thinker develops an attitude that we call pride, and Solomon tells us how destructive this is (Proverbs 16:18). The low thinker, on the other hand, continually puts himself down in such self-depreciating ways that he becomes convinced of his inadequacy. It may well be that circumstances have led him to believe a lie. It is much like being brainwashed by the pressures of life. But the fact remains, God made none of us inadequate. A person acts inadequately only if he is convinced that is the way he should respond, even if it is a delusion (2 Thessalonians 2:11).

The sober thinker, on the other hand, is realistic about himself. He is neither proud nor self-depreciating. He takes himself to be what he is because he knows who he is in God.

Attitudes set the stage for responding, so it is in

observing a person's behavior that we know what he is thinking.

The high thinker with the attitude of pride behaves with a superior air. He is like a man my father-in-law used to talk about: "I would like to buy him for what he is worth and sell him for what he thinks he is worth." The low thinker, on the other hand, takes on the behavior of inferiority. He believes he is inadequate so he behaves in ways that support his feelings.

The sober thinker falls for neither of these faulty mechanisms. The sober thinker with a realistic attitude will treat others as equal, neither better nor less worthy. It is the sober thinker who responds as Paul instructed. (Portions of this section were adapted from Norman Wakefield, *Building Self-Esteem in the Family* [Elgin, IL: David C. Cook Publishing Co., 1977].)

Sacrificial Living

How does sober thinking come about? Romans 12:1,2 explains it. Paul pleads, on the basis of the mercies that God has already extended to the believer, for us to respond totally to Him. The presenting of the body in this passage incorporates the entire personality—all of you. How? As a sacrifice—not to be slaughtered, but to be set aside and dedicated to sacrificial service. Paul sees this as no more than reasonable service in comparison with the sacrifice of Christ and the Father (John 3:16,17).

There are two dimensions to the sacrifice: conform not and be transformed. The word *conformed* means "cut out by the pattern of." In essence, Paul is saying: be not cut out by the

31

pattern of this world, but be "transformed." *Metamorphosis* is the Greek word for "transformed." It means to be completely changed. It can be illustrated by the ugly caterpillar, which spins itself into a cocoon only to emerge as a beautiful butterfly. The change is obvious to all who have viewed the transformation.

It is interesting to note that the word *metamorphosis* is translated "transfigured" in Mark 9:2. There was an aura about the transformed Christ in the Transfiguration. This is also true of the changed life of the living sacrifice who is learning to think soberly.

How does this transformation take place? By the renewing of the mind. It is your perception of what is going on that determines your attitude and your response. Crabb says: "How a person mentally *evaluates* an event determines how he *feels* about that event and how he will *behave* in response to it."(Lawrence J. Crabb, Jr., *Effective Biblical Counseling* [Grand Rapids: Zondervan Publishing House, 1977], pp. 88,89,108). This leads Crabb to conclude that transformed living depends on the renewing of the mind.

Let the Holy Spirit lead you into a new way of thinking, and you will find a new way of behaving. When you do, you will like the new kind of feeling that you get.

It is as we learn to think as Jesus thought that we develop the thought patterns that bring the attitudes and behavior that exalt Christ. Kenneth Taylor translates Philippians 2:5 this way: "Your attitude should be the kind that was shown us by Jesus Christ" (*The Living Bible*).

4

Examining Your Options

Option One: Singleness

Since everyone is born single and will remain single for a good part of life, it is wise to look at the advantages of remaining single. There are advantages to be explored while enjoying the single years, even if you plan to be married at some later date.

Single people have fewer restrictions on their lives. They have more freedom of time and movement simply because their lives are not as meshed with others who depend on them for maintenance. This gives them more flexibility when deciding where they will live, the kind of job they will have, and what they will do with their nonworking hours. Singles also have fewer restrictions on their money and can use their resources more deliberately.

Because of these freedoms of movement and involvement, singles have more flexibility in Christian service. They have more unrestricted opportunities to serve God in individually unique ways. Singleness also allows them more money to devote to self-improvement and advancement through hobbies and recreation. And, of course, they have more freedom to grow professionally by continuing their education, attending workshops and conventions, and working overtime when necessary.

But there are limitations to being single too. Singles frequently have problems with loneliness. This need not be a major problem to the individual who knows who he is, has made his commitment to Christ, and has chosen his career realistically. Loneliness can be as much of a problem in marriage as it is in singleness. However, the single person does have much freedom in choosing how to handle the time he has alone, so he need not succumb to the problems of loneliness.

Some individuals who live alone do not eat properly simply because they do not take the time to prepare nutritious meals. This should not be, however, for the body, as the temple of the Holy Spirit, needs to be nourished and taken care of at all times (1 Corinthians 6:19,20).

Unless they choose to share an apartment with a roommate, there is no one to help singles with the chores of daily living. The person who is creative as a single, however, will take pride in his surroundings and strive at all times to keep his place orderly and attractive. A person's living area is a reflection of his self-concept—it shows how much respect he has for himself.

Some singles express difficulty in establishing a close companionship with someone else, especially someone of the complementary sex. This need not be, however, if the single extends himself into the lives of others and responds to them affectionately, as discussed in chapter 3. Some singles complain of the stigma society places on being unmarried. This need not be a problem if the single is objective about life and in touch with his real world. After all, he is the one who has made the choice to remain single.

There are two real liabilities that singles must face. They have to learn how to handle their normal sexual desires and they do not have the joy of rearing their own children. But, as in any decision, these are part of the package. When singleness is elected, these deprivations go along with the choice and must be handled in keeping with spiritual values.

Option Two: Marriage

Just as there are benefits to being single, there are also benefits to being married. In marriage there is the opportunity for companionship. This is the first major reason for Christian marriage and is a very real benefit. There is someone to come home to; someone with whom to share the responsibilities of household chores. When a married couple remain close friends, they have each other to assist in all of the dimensions of personality growth and professional advancement.

A distinct advantage of marriage is the privilege of sexual lovemaking with a person who is deeply loved and viewed as a gift from God (Hebrews 13:4). With the sexual privilege in marriage comes the potential for bearing and rearing children (Psalm 127:3-5).

Studies indicate that it is not the presence or absence of children in marriage that makes for happiness. Rather, it is the attitude of the partners toward children. If both want children and they cannot have them for reasons of sterility, it really does not matter. The fact that both wanted children and were willing to participate in parenting binds them together harmoniously. If one wants children and the other does not, however, these divergent attitudes generate problems and introduce unhappiness into the relationship.

Still, as with any good thing, there are limitations that are part of marriage. Married individuals have more restrictions on their time, money, and freedom of movement. They must keep the needs of the entire family uppermost in their planning, so they are not free to do just as they please. The money earned by one wage earner must be distributed among all who are depending on him for survival. This is not as much of a problem when both the husband and wife are working, but it is always wise to consider both incomes as "ours" rather than "his" and "hers."

Time is at a premium for the married couple. They must take each other and the children into consideration and plan equitably for all concerned. The matters of nights out and recreation must be planned without neglecting home responsibilities. The place where the couple will live and the kind of community in which they will accept employment must be governed by what would be best for the whole family, not just one member of the family.

From the Christian service aspect, marriage may influence how free each partner is to work for the Lord. If for some reason the marriage is not compatible, friction will build pressures in the relationship that will inhibit freedom for Christian service. God never asks us to neglect our family or our marriage to serve Him, so the family will influence the degree of involvement in Christian service.

Which Does God Prefer?

Scripture teaches that both singleness and marriage are gifts from God (1 Corinthians 7:7). Jesus and Paul set examples of what it is like to be free for Christian service because they were not attached to marriage and family responsibilities. Paul acknowledged the problem of sexual tension in the unmarried and said that if the frustration is too great, it is better to marry a Christian spouse than fall into sexual sin (1 Corinthians 7:8,9,28).

We know Peter was married because Jesus healed the disciple's mother-in-law (Matthew 8:14,15). What Peter has to say to the wife married to an unbelieving husband takes on special meaning when viewed from Peter's standpoint as a married man whose Christian service took him away from home frequently (1 Peter 3:1-7).

We do not know too much about the marital status of other leaders in the New Testament church. We can assume, however, that Timothy followed Paul's instructions about a pastor being married and keeping his children under subjection (1 Timothy 3:1-7).

Each individual needs to seek God's specific witness as to whether the gift of singleness or the gift of marriage is for him. For most, however, the gift of singleness needs to be examined fully in preparation for total fulfillment in marriage. Unless a person learns to enjoy singleness thoroughly, marriage will have unnecessary complications. Happiness cannot be found in a relationship alone; happiness must be within the individual who is entering into the relationship.

It is evident that the single person has more freedom to serve God because he has less demands on his time, energy, and resources. But both the single and married life-styles are approved by God, and His Word has directions for successful living in either life-style.

Should you be inclined to consider the gift of singleness, Wright and Inmon have some good advice:

> If you think singleness is for you, try it for a specific period of time. (Go for one year without a date, devoting your normal dating time to serving God.) If you fail, there should be no thought of having fallen out of favor of God. This is just an experiment. It is similar to trying to go to the mission field and finding you can't. You can still serve God effectively wherever you are. However, you should be as open to God's call to single living as you are to any other call He might give you. (H. Norman Wright and Marvin Inmon, *A Guidebook to Dating, Waiting, and Choosing a Mate* [Irvine, CA: Harvest House Publishers, 1978], p. 11.)

The Bible also teaches that deep personal relationships with members of both sexes should be part of the Christian's life, whether married or single. We must reject the world's assumption that a deep personal friendship with a member of the opposite sex must become a physical relationship. This is also true of members of the same sex.

The relationship between Jesus and His friends in Bethany (Mary, Martha, and Lazarus) was free from sexual overtones (Luke 10:38-42; John 11:1-

46; 12:1-3), as were the friendships between Deborah and Barak (Judges 4; 5), Peter and Dorcas (Acts 9:36-43), and Paul and his tentmaker colleagues Priscilla and Aquila (Acts 18:1-21; Romans 16:3; 1 Corinthians 16:19; 2 Timothy 4:19).

The advantages of extending the period of singleness and delaying marriage are also pointed out by Wright and Inmon:

> Studies of *Who's Who* have shown that successful people usually marry later in life than others in their age bracket. Thus postponing marriage until a person's education is complete and he or she has a start in a profession is a definite advantage. These people also usually have better marriages because they are more mature, know what they want out of life, and have a sound financial base on which to start the marriage. *(A Guidebook to Dating, Waiting, and Choosing a Mate,* p. 11.)

Societal Pressure

The further you move into your adult years, the more pressure there is from society to marry. Frequently, family members, especially some mothers and grandmothers, begin to pressure the single by asking questions. When you see your friends getting married it is easy to feel left out, since we live in a couple-oriented society. The mass media are geared to marriage situations, although often the single-parent family rather than the traditional family is also featured.

With its perverted view toward sexuality, the world assumes it is impossible to live without sexual involvement. Eyebrows are frequently raised toward singles, as people wonder how they handle their sexuality.

A single may always wonder what it would be

like to be married. This can leave him with a feeling of having missed something in life. On the other hand, there are many marrieds who wonder if it would not have been better to remain single than to be involved in the complications of a marriage that is not fulfilling. After all, singles can always get married, but marrieds can never become virgin singles again.

I remember a friend in college who had reached her 21st birthday and, as a nondating single, bemoaned, "I know God made me a man somewhere, but he must have died when he was a baby!" She later went back home, got a good job, and became a faithful worker in her church. When she was in her midtwenties, she met a young man who started attending the church. He had been so busy in graduate school preparing himself for his career that he had not dated much. After a reasonably long courtship they were married. She confided to me later that just as she had accepted her singleness her "prince charming" appeared and swept her off her feet.

Freedom to Choose

The choice is yours. If you want to find fulfillment as a person, seek God and His will first (Matthew 6:33). As you explore the dimensions of singleness, you will find there is so much you can do for the Lord and His people with your freedoms. If, on the other hand, you feel you need companionship and marriage, put your love life on the altar (Philippians 4:5-8).

Paul says you should let your "blessed reasonableness" (moderation) be obvious to all who know you. Why? Because Christ's coming is at hand. All decisions concerning singleness or marriage should be made in anticipation of His imminent return.

If you want marriage, let the Lord know about it. There are three parts to this reasonable request: prayer, supplication, and thanksgiving. This simply means to state your case and then continue to wait on the Lord to ascertain His will. At all times, your petition needs to be overlaid with thanksgiving and submission to His divine will, as you let Him reveal to you His highest order life-style for you.

When you have done this, He will fill you with His peace. Notice that He will fill your *heart* and *mind* with peace. Remember from Mark 12:30 how you are to love God with your heart, soul, mind, and strength? In Philippians, Paul promises that God will keep your heart and mind filled with peace as long as you are asking for His will with thanksgiving. Your heart and mind include all of your thinking powers, so this means you will sense His presence in all dimensions of your thought life.

Since thoughts grow into attitudes, which are evident only in actions, the evidence of the peace of the Lord will be seen in your life if you are presenting your love life to Him. But, the choice is up to you.

5

Different but Compatible

Equally Unique

"So God created man in his own image, in the image of God created he him; male and female created he them." With these words from Genesis 1:27, Moses states God's case for the differences designed by the Creator in His most highly prized handiwork.

It is just a simple statement of fact that God made both male and female compatibly different so that in marriage they could function as a unit (Genesis 2:24,25). That the male is different from the female is obvious from the moment of birth. This does not make one superior to the other, just different.

When we speak of the sexes, we are referring to the two types of bodies God made: male and female. The psychological dimension of sexuality is called gender. It is assumed that the person in a male body will develop masculine traits or gender identifications; it is assumed that the female will develop feminine traits as an expression of her gender identification. The person who does not make the kind of gender identification that is in keeping with his sexual body design develops problems with homosexuality or may even seek transsexual surgery. It is important that boys be reared to be comfortable with masculine roles and girls with feminine roles. Yet, men need to learn to be tender as well as tough, and girls need to be able to be assertive when it is appropriate.

Physical Differences

The most obvious difference between the sexes is size. Men are usually larger than women and husbands are expected to be larger than their wives.

The male skeleton is larger than that of the female and more heavily constructed. It is also rougher in order to accommodate larger muscles, which give men a stronger, more muscular, athletic build. This is the result of the male hormones, which are present from birth but accelerate during the teen years. The muscle and bone structure of the male makes men capable of handling more physical stress and enduring more prolonged stimulation.

The female body is equipped to make tremendous physiological adjustments. The pelvis, for instance, is broader and more shallow than that of the male to accommodate the process of childbearing. The hormones of the female body accent bodily configurations during adolescence, enhancing the female's attractiveness to the male.

There is a difference in how the normal male and female interpret their sex drives. The male expresses considerably more interest in sex, characterized by a greater sense of urgency. He is more sexually sensitive and responds more spontaneously to sexual stimuli. The complication for the single male is that his sex drive usually reaches its peak of urgency between ages 19 and 20. The female, on the other hand, may not experience sexual urgency before age 30.

The single Christian who learns to channel his sexual energies into the nonsexual activities of sublimation will be able to maintain his virginity without undue stress and still have no difficulty functioning sexually when and if he marries at a later age. If he does not learn how to channel his sexual energies, however, he will find himself plagued by the guilt of sin that comes from sexual indulgence.

Emotional Differences

Henry Bowman, a Christian sociologist, points out that men are usually more aggressive than women and vent their aggressiveness in sports, business, and warfare. Women, on the other hand, are said to be more adaptable to new situations. Both seem to have sensitive egos but manifest them in different ways. Pressures from society for men to perform vocationally and sexually place unique stress on the male ego, making it exceptionally fragile and vulnerable.

It has been said that women are more emotional than men but that men are more intellectual and logical; that men reason, while women feel. Recent studies do not support this observation, however, and suggest that the observed differences are a matter of the type of emotion being expressed and the degree of freedom allowed.

Society has made women feel freer to express their emotions, especially fear, anger, sadness, and affection. Men, taught as boys that they shouldn't cry, find it harder as adults to display honest emotions or affection. Such inhibitions greatly affect marital adjustments and relationships with children.

In dealing with other people, men have a tendency to be straightforward and, at times, blunt. Women, on the other hand, tend to be more indirect and approach a subject more obliquely. This characteristic is one of the problems faced in communication between the sexes.

Bowman further highlights the subtle emotional factors that emerge between singles who show interest in each other:

> In courtship men tend to assume the role of pursuer while women tend to assume the role of pursued. Women respond favorably to pursuit by men; men usually respond unfavorably to pursuit by women. This difference is probably the result of both biological and cultural factors. When one sex attempts a reversal of role, the other is inclined to resent it. Women almost unconsciously assume the role of the pursued, but not actually to the point of escape. They know that, with custom and men being what they are, to seem to run away invites pursuit. Men's interest in women, on the other hand, is exhibited more directly, more aggressively, and more obviously. (Henry A. Bowman, *Marriage for Moderns* [New York: McGraw-Hill Book Company, 1974], p. 15.)

Role Expectations

With all of the obvious differences between the sexes, a single person looking toward marriage needs to be honest with himself and his dates as to what kind of expectations he has from a budding romance. In some subcultures certain roles are performed almost exclusively by the male or female. These expectations must be openly discussed early in the dating relationship or problems will emerge that could have been averted.

A potential wife needs to be aware of what a man must think of himself to survive in his culture. She must be alert to the demands his job puts on him and what he must be willing to endure in order to survive and advance in his profession. Unless a man is fulfilled vocationally, he will begin to function inadequately as a worker and a husband. A man's vocation is inseparable from his identity.

A potential husband, on the other hand, needs to be aware that his wife will want him to share his worries with her and not keep his feelings to himself. A wife hopes her husband will admire her for her competencies and praise her for her creative efforts in appearance and the things she does just for him. She also hopes her husband will draw on her intelligence and sensitivity. Here is where the man must accept the fact that men think differently from women but it is through different perceptions that new insights can be discovered.

A wife hopes her husband will express his affection with words as well as with thoughtful surprises. It is what Henry Drummond calls "love in trifles," love in the little things.

Both male and female in a budding relationship must respect each other's individuality. To marry a person with the intent of changing him, as we have already discussed, is self-defeating. Each member of the marriage must be able to grow straight and tall without leaning on or being absorbed into the other. To lose identity in a relationship is fatal.

When it gets to the specifics of washing and ironing, doing dishes and vacuuming, the couple must be honest about their expectations. The division of household chores will usually be based on what the couple's parents did. One of the most important aspects of courtship is coming to terms with role definitions and defining them so there will be no secret expectations to emerge later in the relationship. Total honesty from the beginning of the relationship is the best policy, no matter how difficult broaching the subject may appear to be.

Examining Compatibilities

With so many obvious differences between the sexes it may seem that there is no basis for compatibility between them. God said He was making Eve to be a "help meet" for Adam, or a helper to meet his needs (Genesis 2:18). It is in looking at the dimensions of helping relationships that compatibilities emerge. Any couple should discuss early in their dating relationship the things they have in common. The more areas they share to begin with, the easier it will be to relate. Here are some areas that should be explored for their similarities.

1. *Hobbies and recreation.* What do you do with your leisure time? What do you do to enrich yourself and maintain good physical and emotional health? It is important for a dating couple to have a number of leisure time activities that they both

enjoy. However, they both need not be equal competitors in these events. A man who enjoys contact sports, for instance, needs to be especially careful not to expect a spectator girl friend to get as much fun out of the game as he does. If she is constantly a spectator in his activities, her enthusiasm will dwindle with monotony.

It is also appropriate to maintain some leisure activities to be done in solitude so that everything does not require dual participation. Crafts, art, music, gardening, reading, and such activities can be enriching whether done together or alone.

2. *Vocations.* Vocational compatibility needs to be assured. It is not suggested that both husband and wife should be pursuing similar careers. In fact, too much career involvement could grow into competition. Couples must avoid competing with each other for professional status. There is nothing wrong with a husband and wife both being in the medical field, for instance, but it would be devastating to the marriage if both were aspiring to become the chief of staff at a hospital. Having two lawyers in the family is all right, but they should not both be running for the same judgeship or political appointment.

In vocational considerations, it is important to see the career of the homemaker and housewife as a viable option. If a woman wants to prepare for a career, she should be encouraged to do so. If she wants to concentrate on a marriage and family, that is an exalted career, one defined at the dawn of creation. What is crucial is that both the husband and wife share the same expectations and that one does not force a personal choice on the other.

Many women today prepare for a career and work for a while, then take time off to raise a family. Later, when the children are well into school, they may return to their career. In this type of choice, plans must be made for the woman to keep current in her career during the child-rearing years and to get whatever refresher education is necessary for reentering the work field after being out of it for a while.

Both husband and wife must be free to grow with their professions. If not, stagnation will result and that is devastating to a marital relationship.

3. *Budgeting.* Compatibility in money matters is very important. Early in your relationship you must start looking at how you value money and what it buys. Where there is a discrepancy in the value placed on money there will be friction in the marriage (1 Timothy 6:6; Hebrews 13:5). One of the difficult tasks of courtship is taking the time and energy to share attitudes related to money and establishing a budget. If you can't stay within a budget while living alone, you will never make it financially in a marriage. You should practice money management by setting a budget for dating and see how you react to its limitations. Be reasonable: two can*not* live as cheaply as one!

4. *Age.* Compatibility in age contributes to harmony in a relationship. Usually the male will be slightly older than the female, but there are no hard-and-fast rules. What is important is that they share a common perspective on life in relation to vitality and energy. Where there is a wide age discrepancy the younger person frequently is expected to age quickly or act older than his

years. Later he may be tempted to look back on his lost youth. However, age is not always related to the calendar and a person may be older than his years or younger than the calendar indicates.

5. *Socioeconomic status.* Common social and economic backgrounds contribute to compatibility. Vast differences between the poor and wealthy seldom stand the pressures of marriage. Many illustrations can be taken from the society pages of the newspaper to illustrate the danger of marrying either too far above or below the lifestyle to which the person has grown accustomed.

6. *Race.* The Bible has nothing to say about interracial marriage. Thus, the same guidelines are offered here as in the other parts of the discussion: the more compatibility in the relationship, the greater the chance for success. Racial, ethnic, and even strong cultural differences between the couple will introject tensions into the relationship.

7. *Spiritual goals.* This is probably the most important of the compatibilities to be explored in dating. It is dangerous to consider marriage with a person who is not spiritually compatible. That is why it is important for Christians to date only Christians (2 Corinthians 6:14). Furthermore, if you feel the call of God on your life you must be even more selective. You should date only those who are seeking an intimate relationship with Christ and are striving to be led by the Holy Spirit into Christian service. Just anyone is not good enough for you—you are special!

6

Developing Relationships

Broadening Your Perspective

You were born into a family. It is from this family base that your relationships broaden to include the world in which you live. Then your relationships narrow again as you become involved with romantic considerations.

At birth each person is capable of an emotion called excitement. Self-love is the first expression of this primitive emotion as the child controls his environment with smiles and cries. This self-love is not wrong, it is only an expression of concern for physical and emotional comforts. Normally, self-love broadens to include first the mother and then the father in the beginnings of what will become unconditional love and acceptance. Love broadens within the family to include siblings and other family members. As it does, it becomes less exclusive and more accepting.

Feelings of affection continue to broaden, becoming less intense, to include other relatives in the extended family. Next, love enlarges to include peers of the same sex, then people in the neighborhood, until it finally encompasses all mankind in what the Bible calls "brotherly love"

(Romans 12:10; 1 Thessalonians 4:9; Hebrews 13:1).

Love for others in the community brings with it a sense of responsibility for one's own behavior as it relates to the care of and respect for others. It is marked by a desire to make life better for others, to have a positive influence on their lives. Unlike romantic love or family love, brotherly love is not exclusive. It is the approach to life that accepts others and finds expression in the injunction from Jesus to love your neighbor as yourself (Mark 12:31).

It is essential for a person to make the transition from self-love through family love to community love in order to have a healthy attitude toward God and His universe. Until you have freed yourself from the ties of self-love and parental love, you will not be able to "leave and cleave" as Scripture requires (Genesis 2:24; Matthew 19:4,5). (Portions of this section were adapted from Henry R. Brandt and Homer E. Dowdy, *Building a Christian Home* [Wheaton, IL: Scripture Press, 1960], p. 139.)

Narrowing Your Perspective

As you learn to look outside yourself, to take your place as a part of God's total creation, and to accept the universe in which He has placed you, you can start narrowing your perspective in human relationships. In narrowing your perspective, you concentrate your attention more deliberately toward developing meaningful personal relationships. The ease with which this is done will depend on how well the broadening experience has been accomplished.

Moving in broad friendship circles with members of both sexes gives maximum opportunity for developing social skills and learning the arts of dating. It is in these groups, which emerge through school, church, and community activities, that many lasting friendships develop.

Singles who are too eager to establish a romantic relationship are tempted to rush into dating activities at an early age, and often they encounter complications. They either get involved by going too far too fast or the relationship dies a premature death from overexposure. The temptation of dating too early or compulsively is to get married before you are ready for marriage. Unhappiness results.

The recommendation at this point is simple: prolong friendships and casual dating within Christian groups so there will be sufficient opportunity to get acquainted with a variety of personalities. The longer friendships remain nonbinding, the better chance you have of becoming the right person for a mature relationship, and the more opportunities there will be for finding the right kind of partners from among whom to make romantic choices.

As friendships in groups become selective, moving to double dating is profitable. In double dating, continued skill in social relationships can be developed without putting undue pressure on the dating couple. By narrowing the circle of friendships you maximize the interaction with each other, but you also cut off opportunities for meeting new potential dates. This can be partly alleviated by double dating with a variety of other couples.

Single dating should be a prolonged period in developing relationships. It is in single dating that each person has a chance to observe what is happening to himself and to relate effectively with another person.

Single dating should be enjoyed with a variety of different individuals. There is no reason to feel obligated to continue a dating relationship with one person, however, if discoveries are made that are not in keeping with your own values. The problem with many young people is that they feel obligated to continue dating a person for fear they would hurt him or her if they broke up. But if you feel you cannot grow creatively in a relationship, it is better to terminate it than to let it go on, waiting for the other to make the move. Honesty requires not leading a person to believe that more is intended than you can honestly give.

Concentrating Your Attention

As single dating options narrow and the scope of interest concentrates on one special person, steady dating emerges. Going steady is very serious business, for it implies that all other options are being cut off in favor of developing this one relationship. Going steady for date security or to have someone available on call is an insult to mature relationships.

A definition may be helpful at this point: dating is delaying marriage; courting is preparing for marriage. Dating includes those behaviors that are part of a friendship that allows you to grow as a person in a variety of social relationships. Courting, on the other hand, begins in steady dating and grows into an engagement. That is why it is so important to conduct early dates so that they are just that, delaying marriage and having a good time with no commitments made or concessions given.

Engagement is a very serious time in a relationship. It declares formally to the whole world that each of you has stopped looking for a mate and is concentrating on preparing to enter marriage with each other. Engagement should never be entered into lightly. On the other hand, it is important to keep alert during the engagement period. If factors emerge that indicate the marriage would be premature or unworkable, it is better to have a broken engagement than a divorce. Engagement is a premarriage arrangement and requires the same fidelity of interest that marriage will demand.

Making a Choice

It is in steady dating that the questions in the previous chapter should be explored. There are also some additional questions that need to be considered as you move from steady dating toward engagement in your courtship.

1. *Family.* Relationships with both of the families are very important. When both families approve of the romance, it is supportive to the relationship. If either set of parents is not favorable, however, it puts a strain on the couple. Whatever the reservations of the parents might be, the couple will be influenced by the lack of united support. One set of parents may be over-possessive. It is at this point that the decisions

involved in "leaving and cleaving" must be made.

Parents sometimes appear to be slow in accepting the development of a relationship between two young people. Their reluctance may be based on personality factors that they feel the young couple are not yet aware of or have been blinded to by infatuation. However, it may also be that the parents have had problems in their relationship with their own parents and find it difficult to adjust to a new generational role.

Whatever the reason behind the reluctance, the young Christian couple would be wise to hold steady and work creatively for good in-law relationships. After all, these are the folks who will someday be grandparents to your children and they will be a major factor in the success of the marriage.

More frequently, the problem is that of timing. Young love can be so compulsively possessive that it moves more rapidly than the parents feel is healthy. They may see that the young couple have not had enough time to explore the dimensions of their relationship and are making premature decisions.

Careful timing of announcements related to engagement and marriage is important to avoid unnecessary parental interference and the resulting heartache. Couples would be advised to delay finalizing dates until the parents can be supportive of the announcement.

2. *Friends.* The influence your friends will be allowed to have in your marriage is a serious consideration. These are friends who have been important to you in your youth and maybe even your childhood. It is important for friendships to

continue after marriage. In dating, then, it is wise to look at each other's friends and see if their influence on the marriage would be constructive. If the friends of a fiancé are objectionable, it may be that an engagement would be premature.

It is true that new friends will be made after the marriage ceremony. However, friends of long standing need not be dropped just because of marriage. Friendships reflect compatibilities and those made after marriage will not be appreciably different from those made during the single years.

3. *Desire for children.* Whether or not you want to have children should be discussed before the engagement. As noted earlier, if both persons want children, it will not really matter whether they have them or not. But, if one wants a child and the other objects to parenthood, it would be disastrous to the marriage. It would be wrong to enter marriage expecting to enjoy parenthood, only to discover that your mate felt negatively toward the prospect or was even reluctant to consider it.

4. *Residence.* Where you are going to live is an important factor to consider. It must be decided in conjunction with your career involvements. In most cases, the town of residence will be determined by the husband's place of employment, since his is usually the primary source of income. However, there are marriages where the choice is based on other considerations. That is why it should be discussed openly and not just be assumed.

Also, the style of housing and furnishings should be discussed. This will reveal both aesthetic tastes and the value placed on material things. A good activity at this time in the relationship is to make a list of the things that would be needed to furnish an apartment and go on a window-shopping spree to get an idea of what it would cost to set up housekeeping. It may well be that renting a furnished apartment will be necessary at the beginning of the marriage.

Moving Toward Intimacy

The goal of narrowing relationships is to move toward greater intimacy. Intimacy must be emotional before it can be achieved successfully in a physical relationship.

Intimacy has been defined as "a developing process over a period of time which brings individuals into close association, contact, and familiarity." Wright and Inmon point out that these are "elements necessary for developing a warm, long-term relationship." Further, "an intimate relationship can be characterized as one in which trust and honesty are evident in all dealings and in which individuals can share their deepest nature (feelings, thoughts, and fears) without fear of undue criticism" (H. Norman Wright and Marvin Inmon, *Preparing Youth for Dating, Courtship, and Marriage* [Irvine, CA: Harvest House Publishers, 1978], p. 22).

Intimacy is a process. It must be nurtured as a treasure of great price. Achieving the capacity for sharing on an intimate level is essential to mature relationships. Its early lessons must be learned in adolescence or later relationships will be hampered. This is why it is important for Christian young people to have ample opportunity for making and maintaining friendships on a broad basis before they start single dating. If they do not learn to be totally honest in early relationships, they will be inhibited in trying to make a commitment later on.

Intimacy is natural. In intimacy, a person is natural at all times. He does not put on airs or make pretenses. He is what he is because that is the way he is. It is in such natural openness that true identity can emerge. Emotional intimacy thrives in an atmosphere that allows the relationship to be free and open, with access to each other without criticism or restraint. "Honesty and trust become the bywords."

Intimacy is nonpossessive. You do not own each other just because you are developing a relationship; you both must feel free to be independent while contributing to the welfare of the other in the relationship. It is when demands are laid on a relationship that it becomes restricted. In true intimacy, you learn to love each other so loosely that you can allow freedom of movement without fear of rejection. This is a mature attitude that requires time to develop, and it is based on an adequate view of who you really are.

Intimacy need not be sexual. Sexual performance is no measure of intimacy. Many couples do not become intimate until after several years of marriage, and some marriages fail because intimacy is not developed. In other cases, the marriage may continue, but be bound together only by some outside motivations, such as "economics," "the children," "religious beliefs," or "for appearance' sake."

Intimacy, as we are examining it from an emotional perspective, is a nonerotic relationship between two people who are totally transparent and open with each other. It results in positive feelings toward self and others and is the basis for lasting friendships.

In a romantic sequence, intimacy allows a relationship to move from being mere acquaintances to a deep friendship. Becoming close friends leads to learning how to give and receive love and how to respond to the deep feelings of intimacy without erotic overtones. It is emotional intimacy that is nurtured in dating and courtship. Within marriage, the physical dimensions of intimacy can be explored successfully, but unless emotional intimacy is achieved before marriage, total happiness in marriage will be an elusive dream.

Recognizing Infatuation

Intimacy allows love to develop. Although intimacy is neither love nor infatuation, it is the atmosphere in which love matures. When a person develops progressively from friendship through dating into the courting behaviors of going steady and becoming engaged, he will learn the difference between infatuation and love.

Bowman points out that "love grows, and all growth requires time." On the other hand, "infatuation may come suddenly." Infatuation is compulsive in nature. The strong urge to love someone becomes fixed on one individual. It is common in adolescence, "when new emotions with which the young person has not yet learned to live" are misunderstood. These emotions are largely the result of physiological development rather than experience.

Infatuation may also be an outgrowth of feelings of insecurity because of perceived unattractiveness or limited dating opportunities. Infatuation dies under stress, but the more true love is exposed to the strain of life the more it pulsates with life.

As friendships mature through the distractions of infatuation, love is born. It is by becoming a loving person, capable of both giving and receiving love, that happiness in interpersonal relationships is discovered. To experience an expanding love is to discover the dimensions of what God is like, for God is love, and His Word teaches us how to become loving individuals.

7

Three Little Words

Defining Love

"I love you!" How cherished these three little words are to both singles and marrieds alike. They represent unconditional acceptance by someone special.

To define love is difficult. *Webster's New World Dictionary of the American Language* gives as the first of nine definitions: "A deep and tender feeling of affection for or attachment or devotion to a person or persons." *The American College Dictionary* lists 14 definitions for love.

Attempts to define love are legion in literature. Montaigne defined love as "an insatiate thirst for enjoying a greedily desired object." He further said that "marriage happens as with cages: the birds without despair to get in and those within despair of getting out." Less pessimistic is the view of Henry Van Dyke, who observed that love is "the heart's immortal thirst to be completely known and all forgiven."

Ben Jonson defined love as "a spiritual coupling of two souls." It was Bellinghausen who saw love as "two souls with a single thought, two hearts that beat as one." Magoun says that love is "the passionate and abiding desire on the part of two or more people to produce together the conditions under which each can be, and spontaneously express, his real self; to produce together an intellectual soil and emotional climate in which each can flourish, far superior to what either could achieve alone" (Alexander Magoun, *Love and Marriage* [New York: Harper & Row Publishers, Inc., 1956], p. 7).

Edith Schaeffer says love is essential to Christian relationships:

> Love is one of the basic commands which the Bible gives us concerning human relationships. Husbands are to love their wives. Christians are to love each other. People who are in the family of the Lord are to love their neighbors (representing the ones who are not believers). We are to love our enemies. Love is a basic ingredient of human relationships which is meant to be taught in the family. (Edith Schaeffer, *What Is a Family?* [Old Tappan, NJ: Fleming H. Revell Co., 1975], p. 88.)

Describing Love

Attempts at describing love have been more successful than trying to define the concept. The best known description of love is given by Paul in 1 Corinthians 13:4-7. He suggests nine component parts that will be present in true love. Love is:

1. *Patient.* Love suffers long; it endures offenses. This is the dimension of love that passively understands and waits for God to right all wrongs.

2. *Kind.* Love is considerate; it seeks actively to give pleasure, helps when hurt, and is distinguished by its tenderness.

3. *Generous.* Love envieth not and is magnanimous with time and energy. It is content, not envious. Love is never jealous of people, time, or accomplishments.

4. *Humble.* Love is not conceited or arrogant. It is not haughty or proud. Love forgets its own acts of kindness and concentrates with appreciation on what the loved one has done.

5. *Courteous.* Love is not ill-mannered or rude, but is polite. Love is not boastful and does not show off or try to impress others. It does not strive to be the center of attention but demonstrates love in little things ("trifles," as Henry Drummond puts it).

6. *Unselfish.* Love knows there is no greatness in things and finds pleasure in giving more than receiving.

7. *Self-controlled.* Love is not irritable, but demonstrates a temperament that is emotionally stable. Love is noted for the absence of anger, hate, and fear. It is void of sullenness, touchiness, and self-righteousness.

8. *Forgiving.* Love is generous, not vindictive or wrathful. Love does not keep a record of wrongs and imputes no ulterior motive to the behavior of another. Love puts the best connotation on every action.

9. *Sincere.* Love is not happy with evil, but is happy when truth prevails. It demonstrates a self-restraint that refuses to take advantage of the faults of others. (For additional commentary on the facets of love, see *The Christ-centered Family* by Raymond T. Brock [Springfield, MO: Gospel Publishing House, 1977], pp. 52-60.)

Levels of Love

Three Greek words are used to describe different levels of love that emerge in romantic relationships: *philia, agape,* and *eros.*

1. *Philia. Philia* is the beginning level of love. It is the brotherly love, the community level of love, that was discussed in the previous chapter. It represents a fondness for a person and implies affection and personal attachment involving sentiment and feeling. The word *Philadelphia,* meaning "city of brotherly love," comes from this Greek word.

Filial love, as it is sometimes called, is emotional, inconsistent, and changeable. It involves mental assent more than commitment. This is the love found in friendships and is not romantic in its expressions. In a good marriage, however, the couple will want to remain friends. To the degree that they do, *philia* will blend into their *agape* relationship.

2. *Agape. Agape* is the highest form of love. Shostrom and Montgomery point out that *agape* "could be translated spontaneous, altruistic love that involves unselfishly willing the highest good of another. It is the love that cherishes, affirms, and respects the uniqueness of another person" (Everett L. Shostrom and Dan Montgomery, *Healing Love* [New York: Bantam Books, 1979], p. 55).

Roberts and Wright add:

> *Agape* is self-giving love, gift love, the love that goes on loving even when the other becomes unlovable. *Agape* love is not just something that happens to you; it's something you make happen. Love is a personal act of commitment. (Wes Roberts and H.

Norman Wright, *Before You Say, "I Do"* [Irvine, CA: Harvest House Publishers, 1978], p. 18.)

Agape love means to love with all the heart—the heart being interpreted in the first century as the seat of affection. It is this highest form of love that is used in 1 Corinthians 13. It is an enduring, mature kind of love. It is the kind of love God has for us and wants us to return to Him. When we say, "Underneath are the everlasting arms...," we are symbolizing the *agape* dimension of love that God has for every person (Deuteronomy 33:27). *Agape* is the love that should permeate a Christian marriage.

3. *Eros.* Although the word *eros* is not in the Biblical text, the force of erotic love is seen throughout the narratives of the Bible. *Eros* is the level of love that seeks sensual pleasure. In the words of Roberts and Wright: "*Eros* is a romantic love, sexual love. It is inspired by the biological structure of human nature. The husband and wife, in a good marriage, will love each other romantically and erotically."

Dating, then, begins with *philia* (brotherly love) and blends into *agape* (selfless) love. The dimensions of *eros* (erotic) love must wait until marriage for fulfillment. To deliberately stimulate erotic feelings in a loved one before marriage is to violate the sanctity of *agape* in the relationship. This is where Christian dating is different from the pattern of the world (Romans 12:2), and requires a different set of attitudes and behaviors.

Validating Love

According to Prescott, it is possible to validate love by examining the following components of true love (adapted from D. A. Prescott, *The Child in the Educative Process* [New York: McGraw-Hill Book Co., 1957], p. 358):

1. *Empathy.* Love involves empathy with a loved one. A person actually enters into the feelings of the loved one and shares intimately the experiences of the other without attempting to influence him or put a label on him. By projecting his own personality into the personality of the loved person, he learns to understand him better and develops the ability to share another's emotions and feelings.

2. *Concern.* Love also involves a deep concern for the welfare, happiness, and growth of the loved one. This loving concern becomes one of the main organizing values in the personality of the one who is experiencing it.

3. *Involvement.* Love motivates action to find ways to make personal resources available to the loved one. The one who loves will take pleasure in enhancing the welfare, happiness, and growth of the loved one. "A loving person is not merely concerned about the beloved's welfare and development, he does something about it."

4. *Acceptance.* The loving person maximizes opportunities to participate in activities that contribute to the welfare, happiness, and growth of the one who is loved. He "also *accepts fully the uniqueness and individuality of the beloved and ... accords (him) full freedom to experience, to act, and to become what he desires to become. A loving person has a nonpossessive respect for the selfhood of the loved one.*"

5. *Prayer support.* In a Christian relationship, a fifth dimension needs to be added to Prescott's

list. The lover in a Christian relationship will support the beloved one with prayer. He will seek through intercession to discover how he can best contribute to the welfare of the loved one, and from Bible study he will determine ways to inspire him to good works (2 Timothy 3:17).

Disguises of Love

Not all forms of love are good. Singles would be wise to be alert to the inferior relationships that masquerade as love. Coleman offers the following unhealthy relationships that disguise themselves as true love (James C. Coleman, *Psychology and Effective Behavior* [Glenview, IL: Scott, Foresman and Co., 1969], pp. 412-416):

1. *"Conditional love."* This is the kind of love an individual gives when he requires that the other person conform to his needs and dictates, but he remains insensitive to the needs of the loved one. Conditional love says, "I will do this for you, if you will do this other thing for me." Or, more dangerously, "If you love me, you will do it." Conditional love is not love at all but disguised manipulation that is usually erotically motivated. The story of Samson and Delilah illustrates this type of disappointing relationship (Judges 16:4-19).

2. *"Possessive love."* In this disguise of love, the loved one is viewed as a possession and treated as private property. It does not allow the freedom that is necessary to develop independently. This possessiveness leads to the "clinging vine" syndrome and the loved one is not allowed to grow freely as a person. Second Samuel 11:1-27

suggests that this is the kind of attitude David had toward Bathsheba.

3. *"Overly romanticized love."* This form of love maintains a constant display of adoration and excitement, almost to the point of worship. It is so idealized that it would be impossible for any human being to live up to its expectations. When the glamour has worn off, the flame ceases to burn. This appears to be the attitude of Michal toward David after the excitement of the Goliath victory had subsided (1 Samuel 18:20,21; 2 Samuel 6:16).

4. *"False or deceitful love."* This disguise of love is probably the most devastating charade love can take. One person professes to love the other and then takes advantage of him for selfish purposes. This kind of love for gratification's sake exploits the loved person and is devastating to a long-term relationship. Deception seems to have been a factor in the relationship of Isaac and Rebekah. It must be remembered, however, that their relationship started with marriage; it never had the opportunity to mature through a period of dating and courtship (Genesis 24:63-67; 27:1 to 28:5).

5. *"Two-against-the-world love."* This is the kind of destructive relationship that emerges when young lovers calculate to establish a marriage against their parents' wishes. Then, when the families accept the marriage and stop fighting it, there is nothing cohesive in the couple's relationship to hold them together. They band together against external pressure, but have nothing to sustain their union when the pressure is off. They find little reason to remain in the marriage if they

have not matured and changed the aggressive base of their relationship.

6. *"Insecure and devaluing love."* Insecure love grows out of a need for personal security. Feeling inadequate, a lover reaches out to grasp onto an object for personal stability. This kind of love is seen in teenage marriages when young people choose marriage as an escape from home, school, a job, or other confrontations with the real adult world. Jealousy permeates this kind of relationship.

7. *"Mutually destructive love."* This is a neurotic form of love "in which the partners undermine and tear each other down." This kind of "relationship appears to be characterized more by hate than by love." This disguise of love drains emotional strength and leaves the relationship fragmented. Ahab and Jezebel seem to have had this kind of relationship (1 Kings 16:30,31; 18:4; 19:1,2; 21:1-25). Unfortunately, this is the kind of home in which their daughter Athaliah grew up (2 Kings 11:1-16).

Love and Feelings

Love is a wonderful feeling, but the source of the feeling needs to be ascertained. Love and sex feel very much alike. Only the mature personality can tell the difference.

Basically, love is an attitude that expresses itself as a rational emotion. As an attitude, love is a function of the parasympathetic nervous system, which has its control center in the brain. As a result, love expresses itself in behavior that is mediated by the will. It can, therefore, tolerate time and space and determine when it will or will not respond. When the attitude of love permeates the whole relationship in Christian romance and marriage, it always functions within a person's value system.

Sex, as a reflexive emotion, is a function of the sympathetic nervous system and is governed by reflex centers in the spinal chord. It is by nature compulsive and does not tolerate time and space easily. Sex is characterized by urgency for fulfillment and does not delay gratification unless the brain intercedes.

Scriptural guidelines need to be injected early into a dating relationship to set the limits of physical involvement. Who sets these limits? You do!

8

Communication in Relationships

Purposeful Communication

One of the basic human gifts that separates mankind from the rest of God's creation is our ability to communicate with each other. Through a system of verbal and nonverbal symbols, we let others know what is going on inside us.

Communication is an "interpersonal transaction," a way of conveying ideas between two or more people. This transaction may be written, spoken, or acted out. Six elements are involved in a complete communication process.

1. *Sender*—the one sending the message in whatever form he wants to communicate.

2. *Message*—the body of information being communicated. Messages may be sent on either the conscious or unconscious level.

3. *Receiver*—the person to whom the message is sent. Eavesdroppers can pick up a message as well as the one for whom it was intended.

4. *Encoding*—the process of preparing the message for sending. It is whatever method the sender decides to use to convey meaning and may be oral, written, or in pantomime.

5. *Decoding*—the process used by the receiver

to make meaning out of the message that has been sent.

6. *Feedback*—the process by which the receiver interprets back to the sender the message he has received.

For instance, two fingers raised in a "V" sign will convey the meaning of victory to those for whom this sign is meaningful. Those who are not familiar with this World War II gesture will miss the message altogether. A single index finger raised skyward has come to mean "one way" within the Christian community, but it is meaningless to those who have attached no meaning to the sign.

On the conscious level, couples need to be aware of the message sent, the message intended, and the message received. How do you know what message has come through? When the receiver responds through feedback such as, "Here is what I think you said...." If the sender agrees, a complete message has been communicated. If, for some reason, the message received is not the one that was intended, feedback gives the opportunity to clarify the situation.

When a message received is not the same as that which was intended by the sender, three problems may be in focus: (1) The sender may not have used the right words, tone, or symbol in sending the message; (2) the receiver may not have been alert enough to receive the message or he has insufficient information to process the complete message; or, (3) the receiver may have preconceived ideas that interfere with his receiving the message in its pure form. The message must be filtered through ideas already in the receiver's mind, and thus may become clouded in meaning. When the message is not understood, feedback is necessary to clarify the situation.

Truth in Love

Paul gives us some excellent help in processing communication patterns among Christians. His injunction is basically: "Speak the truth in love" (see Ephesians 4:15). It is when we learn to speak the truth, the whole truth, and nothing but the truth, that messages come through clearly. There are times, however, when we should give no more truth than necessary to avoid the "sensory overload" that comes from giving more information than can be handled successfully by the receiver.

Norman Wright offers four good suggestions for communicating the truth in love in Christian relationships (*Communication and Conflict Resolution in Marriage* [Elgin, IL: David C. Cook Publishing Co., 1977], pp. 4,5):

1. *"Speak for yourself rather than others."* This means to state how you feel, not what you think others feel, or should feel, in the situation. To do this, you must be specific and avoid generalizations. "Some people wouldn't put up with what I have to put up with" would be communicated better as "I don't think you are being fair with me." The use of "I" to personalize what you are feeling puts the message in straightforward form and helps avoid misunderstanding.

When you do this, you give a statement of the facts as you perceive them. It is true that when you speak this objectively you have to become vulnerable enough to admit your own true feelings, but this is what Christian communication is all about. It forces you to get in touch with your own feelings and allows you to demonstrate Christian honesty and openness.

2. *"Document your observations."* Documenting is describing. It increases your understanding of yourself and gives the other person a much clearer idea of what you are perceiving. "I think you are happy; I can tell by the smile on your face," or "Traffic was unusually heavy and I am tired tonight," gives insight into your feelings. In a bad situation you might say something like this: "Your silence is difficult for me to handle. I really don't know what you are thinking." By stating your feelings, you have given an indication of where your ideas have come from, whether they are valid or not.

3. *"Identify how you feel."* This involves risk because you have no way of predicting how the other person will respond to your message. As noted in the discussion on decisionmaking, you can control only the decision, not its outcome. The same principle applies here: you can identify your feelings but you have no control over how the receiver will respond to your message. So, identify your feelings: "I feel sad," or, "I feel good about what you are doing."

If you need to, use a figure of speech to help you describe your feelings. A figure of speech can make the situation more graphic: "I feel like you have closed the door on me and are not listening to what I am saying"; or, "What you said hit me like a ton of bricks." When action is inspired by your feelings, you can express what you want to do: "I feel like leaping for joy"; or, "I feel like hugging you."

4. *"State what you intend."* This gives you an opportunity to state what your immediate goals or desires are: "Now that I understand how you feel, here is what I am going to do about it."

Messages that tell what you think, see, feel, or intend to do offer maximum opportunity for clear, open communication and avoid a lot of misunderstandings.

Nonverbal Communication

It must be remembered that not all messages are verbal. A lot of what transpires in communication is nonverbal. In fact, it has been estimated that only 7 percent of a complete message is contained in the words. The tone of voice accounts for 38 percent of the message, but the major part, 55 percent, is tied up in nonverbal elements of communication.

Nonverbal aspects of communication take many forms. Body language, for instance, comes through in posture, facial expressions, or gestures. The eyes are very expressive in communicating moods.

Spatial distance (how far you remain away or how close you get) conveys a message. Intimate distance, for instance, is measured from contact to 18 inches away, with personal distance being from 1½ to 4 feet. Social distance stretches out to 12 feet, and beyond that is public distance. It is important in establishing new relationships to be alert to the distance that is comfortable for the other person. When there are cultural differences in the perception of distance and you move closer than is comfortable for the other person, there will be an unconscious shifting of position. For instance, North Americans usually allow more spatial distance in conversation than Latin Americans do.

Touching is a form of communication and can be affectionate or erotic, depending on the place and pressure exerted by the touch. Clothing communicates by color, style, and texture. Smell conveys a message through the choice of colognes or perfumes. The surroundings we create around us also tell a lot about us. The architecture of the house or building in which we live, the objects we use for decoration, and the neatness and order of a home, apartment, or room communicate much about what we think of ourselves.

Time is also a powerful form of nonverbal communication. Whether or not you are punctual says much about what you think of yourself and how much you respect others. There are also cultural differences of which you should be aware. For instance, language structure indicates that Americans move through time whereas time overtakes the Greeks. The Sioux Indians, on the other hand, have no word for time in their language.

Tone of voice is extremely expressive. It can go from loud to soft, and high to low, and the inflections, pauses, and accents used can totally change the meaning of the words used. Take a simple statement such as "I love you." You can convey a variety of meanings, depending on which word you stress. "*I* love you" is very different from "I *love* you" or "I love *you*."

And then there is silence. Silence can express emotions ranging all the way from peaceful to informative to foreboding—depending on the setting in which it occurs.

Listening Skills

If a message is to be received, it must be given undivided attention. Here is where listening skills come in. The following suggestions are helpful in dating and courting relationships. (Adapted from Larry L. Barker, *Communication* [Englewood Cliffs, NJ: Prentice-Hall, Inc., 1978], pp. 57,58.)

1. *Concentrate.* All of your physical and mental energies must be concentrated on listening. This is time-consuming and physically demanding, but it is essential if the message is to be clearly received and understood.

2. *Avoid interrupting.* This is difficult, but it is of vital importance to listen to the entire message without interrupting. Cutting off the flow of conversation interferes with the completeness of the information.

3. *Demonstrate interest.* It is important to be alert to all cues, both verbal and nonverbal, coming from the sender.

4. *Seek areas of agreement.* Look for the elements in the message that are in agreement with your ideas. This will make the reception of the message more positive and help you locate areas of commonality between you and the sender.

5. *Search for true meanings.* Look for the specific meaning of the words used (denotation), rather than their emotional interpretation (con-

notation). It is easy to get hung up on emotional interpretations, or what you *think* a word might imply, and miss the real meaning of the message.

6. *Demonstrate patience.* Since you can listen much faster than the speaker can speak, it is important to exercise patience until the message is complete. Forming conclusions on incomplete information leads to misunderstandings. It is also important to listen completely and not be framing a response while the message is still coming through.

7. *Repress the tendency to respond emotionally.* In too many situations the temptation is to respond emotionally to what is perceived, rather than to react rationally to what has actually been communicated.

8. *Ask questions.* When you don't clearly understand a part of the message, ask for clarification. This can be done directly by asking for additional information or requesting an illustration to clarify the content.

9. *Withhold evaluation.* Again this is difficult at times, but it is important to withhold evaluation of the message, whether it is to be perceived as positive or negative, peaceful or provocative. When evaluation is suspended until all data are in, it will be possible to be more constructive in handling the content of the message.

10. *Provide clear feedback.* To make sure you are interpreting the information accurately, it is important to provide immediate feedback. Rephrase what you have heard from the message and interpreted from the nonverbal elements of the communication.

Again, it is important to emphasize that listening is the most difficult part of communication because of the patience required to withhold response until the message has been formulated and communicated completely.

Resolving Conflict

Inevitably, conflicts arise in relationships. They will continue to arise as long as people are trying to communicate. It is not unusual, therefore, for conflicts to emerge in dating and courting relationships. How couples handle these misunderstandings is a gauge of the effectiveness of their communication.

Norman Wright suggests that conflicts arise as a symptom of something deeper or unfulfilled in the person and this is reflected in the relationship. This source of conflict may fall into one of two categories: needs or values.

Physical needs, the need to feel safe and secure, and the need to love and be loved, are basic and must be fulfilled before a person can turn his attention to relationships and communication patterns.

Values are an outgrowth of our basic view of life. They begin with opinions, which grow into beliefs, which mature into attitudes. As we have already discussed, attitudes become habits of thought that prepare us to respond emotionally to the opportunities of life. Attitudes that are consistent blend together into what we call values. Values become the organizing core of personal identity. It is estimated that a person may have thousands of opinions, hundreds of beliefs, and scores of attitudes, but only a few values. When values are attacked in relationships, or are found not to be compatible, conflict is a natural result.

Unfortunately, most people have not been taught how to resolve conflicts. As a result, when a conflict arises or their values are attacked, they are at a loss to know how to respond adequately.

With practice, a couple can learn to handle a conflict maturely and find that it offers them an opportunity to grow as individuals and gain a better understanding of themselves and others. If a resolution of the conflict is not forthcoming, however, it will hinder the growth of the relationship. The couple will find themselves taking the kind of defensive positions that are inflexible and strain their relationship.

Unresolved conflict ultimately breaks up relationships because continued communication requires an atmosphere conducive to free expression. This does not require surrender for the sake of harmony, but it does demand creatively working through the conflict so that growth can occur and resolution can be achieved.

Jesus gives us some very good guidelines to follow in handling the kinds of conflicts that arise in life (Matthew 5:33-48; 10:16). They are especially applicable to friendship, dating, and courting relationships.

9

Handling Stress

Stress

At every stage in the development of relationships there is stress. Before relationships begin, it is present in the apprehension that is felt when thinking about making a move toward an individual or a group. Stress increases with involvements and with withdrawal from involvements. There is no way to avoid stress in friendship, dating, or courting relationships.

Stress is an emotion that is closely related to thinking. If you perceive that you are in an insecure situation, stress will follow. If you feel insecure and someone reaches out to make you feel accepted, stress subsides and wholeness is experienced. Stress takes many forms. In dating and waiting it is most frequently seen in the form of anxiety, conflict, frustration, or pressure. How you learn to handle the various types of stress before becoming involved in binding relationships will determine the degree of pleasure you will derive from friendship, dating, and engagement. The ability to effectively cope with stress is essential to marital happiness. So *now* is the time to learn how to cope with stress, whether your ultimate goal is singleness or marriage.

Anxiety

Anxiety is an elementary level of stress. It is the feeling of fear or apprehension that arises in relationships with ourselves and with others. Anxiety is also that "unwell" feeling you get when things are not going the way you want them to. It is the feeling you have when you wake up in the morning and don't feel confident to face the day, or the feeling you get when things have been going smoothly and suddenly you are not sure what you should do. The stress of anxiety is universal.

First John 4:18 tells us that "perfect love casteth out fear." When a person feels loved, secure, and accepted, there is no reason for him to experience anxiety, for the acceptance he feels will drive away the feelings of stress.

Much anxiety in relationships, then, results from feelings of insecurity. If you are wanting a relationship to develop more rapidly than it is, you will experience stress. If the relationship is developing too rapidly, stress will also be present. If the progress of the relationship is uneven— moving fast, then slow, then fast again—there will be continued stress simply because you are not in tune with the changing pace.

One of the best ways to cope with stress in romantic relationships is to look at your motives. Are you moving with the flow of the Holy Spirit in the development of the relationship? Or, are you setting goals of your own and feeling unfulfilled because the relationship is not totally under your control?

When you put your love life on the altar, you will be able to accept the developmental pace of a relationship without feeling insecure. Feelings of insecurity wreck Christian relationships because the insecure person has a tendency to reach out and clutch at the object that he thinks he may be losing. As he clutches more firmly, the other one in the relationship feels cornered, constricted, or even crushed. This kind of pressure often brings to an end a relationship that could have been good but never had a chance to develop.

Conflict

Another form of stress is conflict. Conflict is related to decisionmaking. A conflict involves choosing between alternatives that are comparable in strength. The problem is to find which alternative is the better solution to the problem.

Conflicts come in three forms. Some conflicts invite us to *approach* an object or a person, or to make a specific decision. Other options are considered negative and make us want to avoid the choice. These are called *avoidance* options. Then, there are those kinds of complicated situations that have both approach and avoidance elements in them.

Picture yourself standing at the fork of a road. You can turn right or left, but you cannot proceed straight ahead. The *approach-approach* kind of conflict occurs when both options are pleasant. "Shall I date the blond or the brunette?" Both may be equally attractive, but you can date only one at a time.

The *avoidance-avoidance* kind of conflict arises when you have to decide if you are going to wash the car or mow the lawn before a Saturday night date. Both of these unpleasant jobs must be done, so which one will you attack first?

The *approach-avoidance* type of conflict arises when a positive choice includes an element that is negative. "She is a terrific girl, but I can't tolerate her mother!"

There is a subtle element in conflict that frequently goes unnoticed. It is the tendency to not make a choice and thus force others or circumstances to make the decision for you. This, as noted in chapter 1, is called decidophobia, the fear of making choices. To refuse to choose is to surrender your powers of choice.

To cope with conflict, then, it is important to weigh the options, decide which one is the best of the alternatives, and move in that direction. The resolving of the conflict by making a choice will lead to a new set of conflicting alternatives.

As long as there is life there will be conflict. This is where the power of the Holy Spirit directs us through the Word and our own thought processes to make the best choices. It is in the renewing of the mind that we find the good, acceptable, and perfect (complete) will of God (Romans 12:2).

Frustration

How do you feel when life tells you "no" and you cannot do what you want to? This is frustration. It is the feeling you have when you are thwarted in meeting a need or blocked from making a choice. It is like running into a brick wall: you are stymied. Frustration differs from conflict in that conflict always has alternatives. Frustration is simply a dead end and you have to deal with the blockage.

Since you cannot go forward in a frustrating situation, what can you do? Frustration can be faced in three ways. You can give up and stop trying. This is called apathy and involves surrendering to the problem. Another negative way to handle frustration is to withdraw from the situation. There are times when it is appropriate to retreat, but withdrawing from a challenge can become a habit. In romance, however, this can be a viable option when the other person marries, becomes engaged, or clearly declares a lack of interest in continuing the relationship.

A better option in many frustrating situations is to accept the fact that you cannot have what you want when you want it, but to refuse to give up. You lower your profile, become less aggressive, and work constructively for change in the situation. Diplomacy works to your advantage in this reaction to frustration.

When you first start dating and do not have all of the social skills you need, there is a tendency to become apathetic after the first rebuff. However, life is ongoing, and it is wise to recover from the first hurt and stay involved in living. If, on the other hand, you make a few mistakes, even blunders, and feel you have failed miserably, keep working at developing the kinds of skills that will make you acceptable as a friend to both sexes. Later you can concentrate on narrowing your options, but wait until you have developed the kinds of skills that help you to move more comfortably in groups.

If, in a romantic situation, you have allowed yourself to feel deeply and that special person chooses someone else, don't allow yourself to be devastated by the situation. Recognize that he has the right to make the choice. Rejection by one person is not rejection by the human race. Neither is it God who is rejecting you. When you remember that your security is in God, you will have Him to lean on as you withdraw from the situation. It takes time to recover from a hurt, but this allows you time to stabilize your relationship with God.

Frustration is not fatal. It may hurt when you have been sincere and are rejected, but it is not the end of the world. Neither is it your last chance at happiness. And, if you discover that singleness is for you, you can accept it as from the Lord and continue to be a constructive, creative person.

Pressure

Pressure comes from two sources: internal and external. There are times when we put pressure on ourselves by the aspirations and goals we establish. External pressure comes from others and the expectations they put on us. When we experience pressure, we feel impelled to intensify what we are doing or to change the direction in which we are moving.

Competition puts pressure on us. Whether we are competing with others for goals, or with ourselves to beat a previous performance, we experience pressure. In romance, we experience pressure when society sets goals for us or asks us to examine our goals.

"Are you married yet? Why not?" "When are you going to start dating?" These pressures are heavy on college-career young people who are delaying marriage deliberately for educational, vocational, or spiritual reasons. It is under this kind of pressure that many young people have been sidetracked from what the Lord wanted for them. Marrying before graduation or dropping out of college to marry is usually the result of pressure rather than deliberate decisionmaking.

Competition gets worse when it involves friends who aspire to a special relationship with one particular individual. Girls who have been the best of friends can behave like enemies if both of them are attracted to the same young man.

When tension begins to rise, it is wise to stop and take a look inside to see where the pressure is coming from. If it is from your own goals, it may be wise to rethink your aspirations. If it is from other individuals, it may be wise to consider who is the lord of your life. Too many people take the privilege of "playing god" in the lives of others and try to tell them what to do.

One of the beautiful things about being a Christian is that God is our Father and He knows how to communicate with His children. He can speak to us through the Word and through the witness of the Holy Spirit. Take Paul and Barnabas, for instance. The Lord called them into missionary work and revealed to the church what His sovereign will was for them (Acts 13:1-3). The Lord must be the one to call us if He is the one who is going to lead us into the full dimensions of His will for us.

Learn how to listen to the voice of the Lord for yourself and don't wait for others to interpret it for you. There will be times, however, when Christian counsel will help you assess the dimensions of what God is trying to accomplish in your life (Proverbs 11:14). But, the Lord himself will initiate the revelation of His will to you; it does not have to come from someone else.

Life is filled with pressures. It is only as we learn how to handle the pressures of single living that we can cope adequately with the pressures of married life. That is why it is essential to explore all of the dimensions of singleness before starting to deal with the problems of marriage. Anxiety, conflict, frustration, and pressure are part of the human condition and have been since the Fall (Genesis 3:15). The sooner we learn to handle these stresses, the more adequately we can become what the Lord is trying to help us become.

Coping

Learning to adjust to the various forms of stress is essential for singles and marrieds alike. In learning to cope with the stresses of life it is important to recognize that stress is a reality. Our experience with Christ does not protect us from stress, but it equips us to be able to handle it effectively. That is why the whole armor of God is essential (Ephesians 6:10-20).

Coping requires first that we admit the existence of stress. Second, it requires us to look for the source. When we know where the pressure is coming from we can handle it more effectively.

If the pressure is self-imposed by goals and aspirations, we have to be honest with ourselves and adjust our goals so they are within our ability to reach them with God's help (Philippians 4:13). If the pressure is from outside ourselves, we have to evaluate it in the light of what we perceive to be God's will for our lives. Pressure that is distracting must be ignored. Pressure that heightens our concept of God's will must be transformed into motivation, the energy we need to accomplish the work of the Lord (Ecclesiastes 9:10). Pressure to do good works will never be more intense than is comfortable for us, and sometimes it is necessary to inspire us to deeper involvement in the Lord's work.

When we are learning to cope with stress from a Christian perspective, we avoid the temptation to rationalize, explain, or make excuses. We take responsibility for our own behavior. We resist the temptation to withdraw or retreat from the challenges of life. And, at times, we have to resist the temptation to strike out at others.

Within romantic relationships, coping with stress as a Christian allows us the privilege of responding as Christ wants us to in order to fulfill our own lives and enhance the lives of others.

The Word offers us guidelines on how to deal with the normal stresses of life that are exaggerated in dating and preparing for marriage.

1. Examine your thought life and bring it under control (Philippians 2:5; 4:6-9).

2. If you are in error, seek God's forgiveness (Matthew 6:12-15; 11:28; Philippians 1:27). (Note that "conversation" in the Philippians passage means your total life-style.)

3. If you are worrying, turn your future over to God (Isaiah 26:3; John 16:33; Romans 5:11; Hebrews 13:6; 1 Peter 5:7).

4. Work on your love relationship with God and enrich it in daily devotions (Psalm 42:1,2; Mark 12:28-30).

5. Let His love flow through you to all in your sphere of influence (Mark 12:31; 1 John 4:18-20).

10
Expectations in Relationships

Delaying Marriage

In chapter 6 we discussed the importance of broadening interests from the self-centeredness of infancy to the openness of community affiliation. As romantic experiences develop, there is a narrowing of interests and a redefining of relationships. There are several phases through which a normal romance progresses.

1. *Friendship.* This is the level of social awareness in which you have friends of both sexes and of a variety of ages. To learn to be a good friend is a major task of growing up. In friendships, you discover who you are in relationship to other males and females and accept your own identity as a person. It is in knowing who you are that you can reach out and touch others constructively without being erotic.

Friendship is a time of intellectual, emotional, social, and spiritual sharing that turns casual acquaintances into best friends. When the expectations are to give rather than receive, this is a most exciting time in life. A variety of friendships must be explored before you are ready to move to the next stage of a more intimate relationship.

2. *Dating.* Dating is the time in life when you

turn your attention from the group as a whole and concentrate on specific individuals. It is in dating a variety of individuals that you get a look at the varieties of options that are available to you for a long-term romantic choice. You also get a better understanding of yourself. Expectations in dating call for loyalty. This brings more restrictions on your freedom and requires more demonstrations of interest and concern for the one you are currently dating.

When you become aware of the fact that you do not wish to be totally loyal to this one individual, you must make this known so that one person in the relationship does not become more deeply involved than the other. Wise is the young person who enjoys a lot of dating experiences with a variety of eligible individuals.

It is worth mentioning again at this point that dating should be conducted only among those who are eligible for a long-term Christian relationship. To date those outside your value system or become involved with individuals whose lifestyle is not consistent with your goals will only bring heartache to all concerned.

3. *Going steady.* Steady dating should be delayed until well into the dating sequence. To go steady just for security or for fear of being left out is not honest. Going steady should represent a desire to become better acquainted with an individual, but it should not be so compulsive that it eliminates all other options in life. Going steady is a preengagement relationship and places restrictions on all other options in life. Commitments on any level must be honored, even those on the early going-steady level.

Expectations in going steady are loyalty and fidelity. To date someone else when you are committed to going steady is irresponsible.

Preparing for Marriage

Engagement is the stage of formal commitment to another with marriage as the intended goal. Courting behavior evolves during the going-steady period and crystallizes in engagement. The longer a couple have spent in their friendship and dating relationships, the better equipped they will be to handle engagement.

Engagement should not be entered into lightly. It should follow a sequence of maturing experiences in which the individual has a chance to discover his identity and examine what he has to bring to the marriage. The remaining areas of communication and compatibility should be worked out, so that the couple achieve a level of trust and intimacy that makes them confident they can commit themselves to each other in the fear of the Lord for the rest of their lives.

The expectations of engagement include the loyalty and fidelity of earlier relationships plus transparent honesty. A thorough review of your life up to this point is in order. Anything that has happened in the past that could fracture the relationship in the future should be discussed before marriage. If you are going to enter marriage as a Christian, your life's history and goals should be thoroughly explored.

If an impediment exists that could break up the marriage, it would be better for you to discover it during engagement than for it to cause a divorce later. This statement is predicated on the concept

93

of love, which implies that if you love someone you will hide nothing from him deliberately, nor will you do anything to deceive him.

A discussion of roles in marriage is also important. A thorough examination of personal and family role expectations is necessary so there will be no hidden expectations that could emerge later to blight the happiness of the couple.

Reasons for Marriage

Marriage is honorable, Hebrews 13:4 tells us. The idea originated in the mind of God. He performed the first marriage ceremony in the Garden of Eden when He gave Eve to Adam and told them to cleave to each other as long as they both should live (Genesis 2:22-25). It is within Christian marriage that a man and a woman may find total expression of a loving relationship in the presence of God. And, as we noted earlier, it is the goal of most adults.

So, why do Christian adults choose to marry? Several reasons are pertinent.

1. *Companionship.* The first reason for Christian marriage is companionship. Genesis 2:18 tells us that loneliness was the first emotion Adam had in his original created state that he could not handle. So, God created a helper adequate to meet his needs. It is through intellectual and emotional sharing that much pleasure comes in life.

Outside of sleeping and working, most of the time in a marriage is spent in forms of companionship. Both verbal and nonverbal communication are involved. The longer a couple live together, the better they understand each other. As the years progress, they even develop the ability to read each other's body language and anticipate what he or she is thinking or wanting before words are spoken.

It is the loss of companionship that makes death, separation, or divorce so painful. It is not surprising that the survivors of broken relationships appear to be more helpless than they were as unmarried singles. They are also prone to remarry.

2. *Sexual fulfillment.* A special form of *communication* that God has given for expressing love in marriage is sexual gratification. Letha Scanzoni points out that, in the marriage relationship, "sexual intercourse was also designed by God to provide a means of expressing the deep unity a husband and wife feel toward one another. There can be a communion of spirit when there is a union of bodies. This may very well be why the Bible writers frequently used the word 'know' when referring to sexual intercourse (Genesis 4:1,17, 25)." (*Sex Is a Parent Affair* [Glendale, CA: Gospel Light Publications, 1973], pp. 16-21.)

Sexual fulfillment in Christian marriage also brings *pleasure* to both parties as they communicate their love. Mrs. Scanzoni says: "For the Christian couple, sex can be regarded as sacred—if by this we mean set apart from God—desirous of pleasing and experiencing God's blessing in our sex lives as well as in every area of life." But, as John White cautions: "Pleasure is a by-product of life, not a goal" (*Eros Defiled* [Downers Grove, IL: InterVarsity Press, 1977], p. 11).

3. *Procreation.* The third reason for Christian marriage is closely related to the second. Procrea-

tion is separated from sexual fulfillment here to emphasize the fact that childbearing is episodic, whereas sexual pleasure is cyclical. Scripture does not teach that the only time sexual fulfillment is to be enjoyed is when its purpose is to lead to the birth of a child. First Corinthians 7:1-5 points out that sexual expression between a Christian husband and wife should be a regular part of their relationship, but the bringing of children into the world is an occasional, planned event.

4. *Christian witness.* Kenneth Gangel suggests that a fourth reason for Christian marriage is to be a witness to the world of the mystical relationship that exists between Christ and the Church. (See *The Family First* [Minneapolis: His International Service, 1972].) From Ephesians 5:25-32 we learn that Christian couples are to exemplify their submission to God through their behavior in marriage. This involves the husband loving his wife in the same way Christ loved the Church— selflessly and sacrificially. It also includes the response of the wife to the husband in spontaneous, loving submission to the will of God for their lives. Moreover, Scripture requires the father to serve as the priest of the household and to be a model for the children to honor (Ephesians 6:1-4).

5. *Division of labor.* Another reason for marriage is division of labor or role assignments. Since a couple will live together for many years, there needs to be a specific division of labor. Who is going to perform which tasks should be determined specifically before marriage. This needs to be worked out in the engagement period. Division of labor includes such things as: Who will work where? Will both work for a while until the chil-

dren arrive? Who will do the household chores, or will they be divided? Who will manage the budget and pay the bills? Who will take care of home repairs and keep up the car?

Since there are so many varieties of role assignments these days, it is essential for a couple to look carefully and specifically at what they expect each other to do and what they are willing to do to contribute fairly to the welfare of the relationship.

Complementing Each Other

Much has been said about authority and submission in marriage. When the Scriptures are studied in context, it would appear that Paul presents an egalitarian view of Christian marriage (Ephesians 5:2-33; Colossians 3:17-21).

"Submit to one another out of reverence for Christ.... And whatever you do, whether in word or deed, do it all in the name of the Lord Jesus, giving thanks to God the Father through him" (Ephesians 5:21; Colossians 3:17, *NIV*). Paul's admonitions place Christian marriage in a setting of spiritual equality.

In the eyes of Christ, the husband and wife are equal. In Christ there is neither "male nor female," neither "bond nor free" (Galatians 3:28). Both the husband and wife stand as equals before Christ in their relationship to Him, and complementary to each other in Christian marriage.

The wife is told to submit to the leadership of love provided by her husband. To submit means to "yield oneself" and to respond spontaneously to the husband's love. The submission of the Christian wife is not servitude from a position of inferiority. Rather, it is an exalted privilege of responding to the leadership of a husband who is modeling his behavior after Christ in his initiations of love toward her.

The real challenge of this passage is that the husband is commanded to love his wife just like, or to the same degree that, Christ loved the Church (Ephesians 5:25-27). How much did Christ love the Church? Enough to die for her. The goal of the Christian husband, then, is to provide sacrificial, redemptive love for his wife in deep concern for all her needs.

To some, this is a difficult thing to do. So Paul says further: "Husbands ought to love their wives as their own bodies. He who loves his wife loves himself. After all, no one ever hated his own body, but he feeds and cares for it, just as Christ does the church" (Ephesians 5:28,29, *NIV*).

Combining the two ideas, the husband is to follow the leadership of Christ and provide for his wife as selflessly and sacrificially as Christ did when He gave himself for the Church. Moreover, the husband should take care of his wife's material needs at least as well as he cares for his own. "Feeds" and "cares" suggest meeting all her physical and emotional needs.

The husband is commanded to initiate the leadership of love and to be the protector of and provider for the wife. The wife is encouraged to respond spontaneously with the loving submission that inspires the husband to higher dimensions of loving leadership. The result is the perpetual motion of Christian love in the sanctity of marriage until death separates the couple. When this happens, the survivor is free to enter into another marriage if he chooses (Roman 7:3).

Complimenting Each Other

Solomon said: "Whoso findeth a wife findeth a good thing, and obtaineth favor with the LORD" (Proverbs 18:22). To this, Peter adds the concept that the wife is to be honored as a "weaker vessel" (1 Peter 3:7). Again, this is not an allusion that the woman is weak or inferior. Rather, it portrays her as fragile, delicate, special, treasured—like crystal is in comparison to pottery, ironstone, or plastic. On the other hand, she is also pictured as strong, capable, industrious, and a delight to be around (Proverbs 31:10-31). She should be reminded frequently of her specialness.

Dwight Small says:

> When a man and a woman unite in marriage, humanity experiences a restoration to wholeness. The glory of the man is acknowledgment that woman was created for him; the glory of the woman is the acknowledgment that man is incomplete without her. The humility of the woman is the acknowledgment that she was made for man; the humility of the man is the acknowledgment that he is incomplete without her. Both share an equal dignity, honor, and worth. Yes, and each shares a humility before the other, also. Each is necessarily the completion of the other; each is necessarily dependent upon the other. (Dwight H. Small, *Christian: Celebrate Your Sexuality* [Old Tappan, NJ: Fleming H. Revell Co., 1974], p.144.)

A husband and wife who are establishing a complementary relationship will find that in being complimentary to each other their love will grow more rapidly and deeply.

11

Making a Commitment

Becoming Authentic

In the previous chapter we discussed the importance of becoming so totally honest with yourself and another person that you have a "transparent" relationship. This can only come about when you are completely aware of yourself in relationship to God and to others in your environment. Reaching this point of openness in relationships is what is meant by being authentic.

The authentic person is "being a truth." He is the way he is because that is what he is. He does not hide behind disguises or excuses. He is straightforward in all relationships at all times.

Becoming authentic is a process that takes years to develop. Abraham Maslow has given an outline of the steps toward authenticity in his hierarchy of needs. The lower needs must be satisfied and the lower challenges explored before you can move successfully to a higher level. You must move through the "doing motives" of need reduction to the "being motives" of the actualizers before you are ready to make a commitment to either singleness or marriage. (See: Abraham Maslow, *Motivations and Personality* [New York: Harper & Row Publishers, 1954], and *The Farther*

Reaches of Human Nature [New York: Viking Press, 1971].)

Need Reduction

1. *Physical.* All of the life support systems that must be satisfied in order to live are included in this first category. By definition, a person's needs must be satisfied, or he will die. The physical needs include such things as air, food, water, reduction of pain, control of heat and cold—anything that is essential to survival. You cannot work on higher needs unless you are taking care of the body, getting sufficient sleep, and maintaining good physical and emotional hygiene.

2. *Safety.* The need for safety involves being secure and safe from bodily harm or threat of injury while your physical needs continue to be met. You must feel secure in yourself and safe in your environment (home, school, job, neighborhood), if you are to be free to move to higher needs. The Christian has an advantage on this level because he realizes that his safety and security are in Christ (John 10:29).

3. *Love and belonging.* Affiliation needs are on the third level of the hierarchy. These include acceptance, warmth, affection, and approval. It is on this level that you learn to give and receive love. How to care, share, and listen creatively must be learned at this level if positive interpersonal relationships are to emerge in life.

A sense of love and belonging bridges the gap from home to community and moves you from the lower levels of self-centeredness in childhood to the brotherly love of maturing relationships. You need to feel loved at home while reaching out into society for a sense of belongingness in a growing circle of friends.

4. *Self-esteem*. This level includes needs for adequacy, worth, and status, which lead to acceptance by others. It brings with it a feeling of significance as a person, which in turn grows into self-respect. In achieving belongingness, you blend into the crowd to enjoy the joys of affiliation. In self-esteem, however, you stand head and shoulders above the crowd and contribute to their welfare by your training, gifts, and talents.

These four steps toward authenticity are hard work. That is why they are called "doing motives." You have to work at becoming authentic yourself. Neither God nor your parents can do it for you, although God may use others to help you handle these needs so you can mature through the challenges. You have to work and strive for fulfillment, both physiologically and psychologically. But to do so will bring you to the point of being a total person who is free to chart his own destiny within the will of God.

Self-actualization

The top level of needs that Maslow suggests is called *self-actualization*. This represents fulfillment of your growth potential and includes needs for personal growth and realization of potentialities. It is on this level that you achieve your highest potential as a person. No longer are you concerned with handling your physical needs and feeling secure, accepted, loved, or capable of contributing to the welfare of others. You have laid that aside and are flowing in the realization that you do what you do because it is right for you. You become a free-flowing, sharing person. Others reap the benefits of your life and are challenged by what they consider to be your selflessness and dedication.

Self-actualization is the potential of all adults, according to Maslow. Unfortunately, his studies indicate that less than 2 percent of the college-age population achieve this level. It is available to all adults by middle age, but his studies indicate that less than half of the adult population reach this level of maturity.

Becoming a self-actualized person is essential to becoming capable of making the commitment that marriage demands. But there is more. After years of study as a Christian in the behavioral sciences, I have become convinced that there is a level beyond Maslow's self-actualization.

Christ-actualization

I call this higher level Christ-actualization. It is the relationship Paul expressed in Galatians 2:20:

> I am crucified with Christ: nevertheless I live; yet not I, but Christ liveth in me: and the life which I now live in the flesh I live by the faith of the Son of God, who loved me, and gave himself for me.

Christ-actualization moves you beyond what can be achieved by a carnal person to a relationship with Christ that translates the principles of the Kingdom into everyday living (Matthew 5 to 7). It takes one actualized by Christ to be able to love with the Biblical *agape* love, without expectations of return or reward. The life of the Christ-actualizer is more than good mental health. It is a reflection of Christ's life being lived spontaneously because of identification with His death, burial, and resurrection.

Self-actualizers achieve a high level of excellence in living. However, they are limited by the confines on humanity that resulted from the Fall and the penalties assessed on mankind at that time (Genesis 3:15-19). The Christ-actualizer, however, moves beyond these normal limitations by incorporating into his life spiritual values from his identification with the life of Christ.

The process of becoming actualized in Christ includes all of the levels of need reduction presented by Maslow but goes a step further. Although the Christian moves more rapidly through each stage because of the influence of the Word and the power of the Holy Spirit in his life, the main difference between the self-actualizer and the Christ-actualizer is the motivation behind their behavior. The motivation of the Christ-actualizer comes from his identification with Christ in working with Him to build the spiritual kingdom of heaven. The self-actualizer, on the other hand, uses his own resources in trying to create an earthly utopia.

Actualizers make better marriage partners simply because they have learned to resolve the frustrations that fragment relationships. With the Christ-actualizer, Christ becomes the center of the relationship. His presence in dating and courting makes it possible to deal realistically with developing relationships and gives higher goals toward which to strive. It is in moving from "doing motives" to "being motives" that you learn the skills of romantic relationships. Then, each of you is free to become what you are capable of becoming without feeling hindered by unful-filled needs in yourself or the other person.

Obviously, it takes time to bring yourself to this level of commitment. That is why it was empha-sized earlier that marriage is for adults, not chil-dren or teenagers. It does take time, and the more quality time spent learning how to become eligi-ble for a lifetime commitment, the smoother and more exciting will be the total relationship from dating and courting through a lifelong marriage.

Levels of Commitment

1. *Commitment to self.* The previous discussion emphasized the necessity of being committed to yourself and fulfilling your growth potential. The authentic person who can honestly make a commitment to marriage must have explored the dimensions of his own integrity. He must have worked through his value system carefully and es-tablished his priorities and his system of right and wrong. He must have distinguished between the necessities and nonessentials of life. He must be capable of living by these values as a single person before seriously considering marriage. He must demonstrate his authenticity by the goals he makes and how he fulfills them, by the sincerity with which he is responsible for his own behavior, and by the discretion with which he treats others.

A good measure of a person's integrity is to ascertain how closely his life resembles the di-mensions of love in 1 Corinthians 13. The authen-tic person who is capable of a marriage commit-ment to another person will be patient, kind, gen-erous, humble, courteous, unselfish, self-con-trolled, forgiving, and sincere in his daily life (see chapter 7). He will not save these character traits just to impress someone in a romantic relationship.

2. *Commitment to others.* Commitment to others is tied to commitment to ourselves. This is shown in concern for others and their welfare. But you must love (accept, be committed to) yourself before you can love your neighbor (Mark 12:31). To the degree that you do not accept yourself, your ability to be committed to another person in a marital relationship will be impaired.

Of all the reasons given for the increasing number of divorces, it seems the number one cause is lack of commitment. A person must accept himself before he can ask another to accept him. To the degree that he rejects all or part of himself, he will feel that he is being rejected in a relationship. That is why dating and courting must be lengthened sufficiently to allow the couple to handle these problems within themselves and in relationships with others.

3. *Commitment to God.* Jesus put the emphasis here: to love God with your heart, soul, mind, and strength before looking for relationships with others (Mark 12:30). When you are totally committed to God it will show in all the relationships of life. The evidence of His work in your life will be especially visible in the close relationships of dating and courtship.

You are not ready to enter a marriage until you see what the apostle Paul calls the fruit of the Spirit being demonstrated in your life and in the life of the one you are planning to marry. In the context of this book they may be called the fruit of *love*, but these character traits must be in evidence before a commitment to marriage is in order: "love, joy, peace, patience, kindness, goodness, faithfulness, gentleness and self-control" (Galatians 5:22,23, *The Living Bible*).

Impediments to Commitment

There are a number of factors that interfere with the ability to make a clear-cut commitment to marriage. These hurdles must be surmounted before it is safe to enter into marriage.

1. *Immaturity*. Immaturity is a major cause of problems in dating and courting. Unless the lessons of adulthood are learned and the individual progresses through the various levels of needs to actualizing his potential, immaturity will continue to hassle the relationship. Paul points out that the adult must put away his childish ways of thinking and behaving if he is to be mature (1 Corinthians 13:11,12).

Paul Maves offers the following characteristics of an adult that must be taken into account in assessing one's maturity:

(1) The reaching of legal age, (2) completion of his education, (3) physical separation from his parental home, (4) financially self-supporting, (5) capable of making his own decisions, (6) accepts responsibility, (7) sees himself as an adult, (8) is accepted by other adults, (9) seeks the company of other adults. (Paul B. Maves, *Understanding Ourselves as Adults* [Nashville: Abingdon Press, 1959], p. 15.)

Time and experience are the only cures for immaturity. The ability to profit from the experiences of life and to learn vicariously from the experiences of others is essential in the serious business of romance.

107

2. *Family*. Pressures from family members may interfere with commitment. Parents have a subtle way of making demands on a relationship. Sometimes this stems from their lack of fulfillment and their wish to relive their lives in their young. At other times it is the result of overprotectiveness and the inability to let the young be free to chart their own lives. When the extended family is in focus and several generations are making demands, it is even more difficult to be free to make commitments.

It is no wonder that God told Adam and Eve that a couple should leave their mother and father and cleave to each other. And He said this before there were any in-laws to be left! (Genesis 2:24). Jesus reiterated this principle thousands of years later (Matthew 19:5).

Wright and Inmon point out:

> One of the reasons for the emphasis upon you and your present family is that the way you respond to and interact with your parents will have an effect upon your own marriage and in-law relationship. (*A Guidebook to Dating, Waiting, and Choosing a Mate* [Irvine, CA: Harvest House Publishers, 1978], p. 31.)

David Thompson suggests that you take a careful look at your future in-laws and list the important positive and negative traits you have observed, such as "things I especially like about them" and "things I don't particularly like about them." Here are some questions he suggests you respond to in writing (David A. Thompson, *A Premarital Guide for Couples* [Minneapolis: Bethany Fellowship, 1979], p. 30):

a. "What do you believe your future in-laws'

feelings are toward you and your impending marriage into the family?"

b. "What do you see as potential points of conflict with your in-laws (cultural differences, religious differences, etc.)?"

c. "What do you think you can do to resolve these areas of conflict?"

d. "What will be the frequency and the extent of your future in-laws' involvement in your new life as a couple?"

All of these questions must be carefully considered by you and your fiancé before you dare proceed from engagement into marriage.

3. *Vocation.* Since a man and his job are inseparable, vocational demands on a relationship can hinder commitment. It is essential for both the man and the woman in a potential marriage to accept the man's vocational choice. With this comes accepting the educational and social demands that result from the vocational choice.

No one should have to choose between his job and his marriage. The marriage must support the vocational aspirations of both partners. Otherwise, happiness will be incomplete. If necessary, marriage should be delayed until total commitment to the job and its requirements can be accepted without hesitation by both parties.

4. *Social pressures.* Mobility, urbanization, changing views of sexuality, secularization, and materialism all infringe on a marriage. Wise is the couple whose commitment to each other and to God is such that these impediments are resolved during the engagement period.

Yes, the marriage commitment is for a lifetime!

12

Your Contribution to Marriage

Faith in Yourself

When and if you marry, you will contribute three things to the relationship: your faith, your hope, and your capacity for love. Paul says the greatest of these is love (1 Corinthians 13:13). Christian marriage, however, is incomplete without the full dimensions of faith and hope from which love can grow.

To succeed in marriage, you must have faith in yourself. You must have explored the options of both singleness and marriage and determined that marriage is for you. You must have learned to make good decisions and you must be able to stick with them.

You must have explored the dimensions of who you are and become the person God wants you to be. You must have determined what His will is for your life as far as education, vocation, and Christian service are concerned.

You must have accepted your body and learned how to treat it as a temple of the Holy Spirit (1 Corinthians 6:19,20). You must have learned how to handle your sexuality as a single person and also developed the appropriate masculine or feminine life-style.

You must have learned the difference between infatuation, brotherly love, and *agape* love. You must have learned to communicate adequately with others and to listen creatively to them. You must have learned to handle the tensions of life and be able to deal with stress on many levels.

You must have explored the expectations of marriage and be capable of contributing without reservation or inhibition to the total relationship. You must have learned how to resolve the frustrations of life and become an authentic person who has learned the secrets of Christ-actualization.

Having explored these dimensions of living, you must have developed a faith in yourself that gives you the courage to offer yourself to another person without reservation before God, and to commit yourself to that person's total welfare. This commitment must be "for better or worse, for richer or poorer, in sickness and in health, to love and to cherish till death do us part."

Faith in God

Your faith in God needs to be stabilized before you enter marriage. The stronger your religious faith during your early dating experiences, the more you will be able to avoid the temptations of the age (1 Thessalonians 5:22).

Recognizing that all have sinned and come short of the glory of God (Romans 3:23), it is important to accept Christ as Lord and Master, and confess the sins of youthful living (Romans 10:9,10; Hebrews 11:6; 1 John 1:8-10).

The basis of your faith is found in the Word of God (Romans 10:17). As you study God's Word and maintain a consistent devotional life, your relationship with Him grows (2 Timothy 2:15). You learn that the Scriptures were given by God and are designed to teach you what God wants you to know about His doctrine (basis of faith), reproof (guidance to avoid problems in life), correction (discipline for wrongdoing), and instruction (teachings that give new insights into how to handle old problems) (2 Timothy 3:16,17). The more you study, the more you will realize that the Word of God is valuable when hidden in the heart, and it will become like a light to illumine life's pathway (Psalm 119:11,105).

You will move from faith in His teachings to exercising faith in daily living. This will bring the will of God into the everyday situations of life and allow you to experience what it means to walk in the Spirit (Romans 8:1,2).

Marriage is a marvelous place for the application of faith. The Lord can show a couple how to handle problems and misunderstandings. He can show them how to balance the budget and stretch what is on hand until new resources are found (1 Kings 17:12-14). As sovereign of circumstances, He is able to bring to pass in life those things that are necessary for our well-being, and it is His good pleasure to do so (Matthew 6:25-34).

Faithfulness to God

Another dimension of the faith you bring to marriage is your faithfulness to God. This involves all aspects of Christian service. It begins with your tithe.

The first item to be included in the budget of any newly married couple is the tithe (10 percent of all sources of revenue) which belongs to the

Lord (Leviticus 27:30; Deuteronomy 12:5-7; 14:22-29; Proverbs 3:5,6; Malachi 3:8-10; Mark 12:17; 1 Corinthians 16:2).

Many young couples who have been inconsistent in tithing as singles find it difficult to start tithing as one of the initial acts of marriage. Such casualness in their faithfulness to the Lord is usually revealed when their relationship begins to flounder and they reach out for help. One of the first things a Christian marriage counselor will do at this point is to help the couple get their finances in order with their spiritual commitment. It is amazing how the total relationship begins to improve when God's work is put in its rightful place in the budget.

Your testimony is an important demonstration of your faithfulness to God. It is in witnessing of Him to others that we learn how to express our love and gratitude for Him. With the new friendships that come with marriage, there are more opportunities and people with whom to share the good news of Christ. Family members, friends, and colleagues at work, in addition to the whole scope of recreational friends, provide ample opportunities for witnessing.

Whatever forms of Christian service were enjoyed as a single should continue to be enjoyed in marriage. In addition, the fact that you are now a part of a couple opens new vistas of Christian service for you. Much of the New Testament witnessing was done in teams of two. Witnessing is natural for couples.

Christian service assignments can be handled effectively as a team. Team teaching a Sunday school class or cosponsoring a group activity can be added to your scope of involvement. Also, you now have a living room of your own in which you can entertain for Bible study and prayer. You should not only continue to use your time and talents for the Lord, but also enlarge the scope of your involvement.

Hope for the Future

The hope you bring to a marriage includes your goals and expectations. The most obvious expression of this hope is in your vocation. Having discovered in singleness the gifts and talents the Lord has given to you, you must continue to develop them in marriage.

Strive to grow in your profession. Whatever career you have chosen, give it your best. This requires that you continue to develop the skills of your vocation and become a better worker, performing your task as unto the Lord (Ephesians 6:5-9; Colossians 3:22-25).

If both husband and wife are working, due consideration should be given to the special pressures that are on each as a result of this choice. When both are working outside the home, it is only fair that the home work be split down the middle and that each partner have specific assignments to be carried out so that the equality of the relationship can be maintained.

When a wife suspends work to have a family but plans to reenter the job market later, it is essential that she keep abreast of what is going on in her field. Otherwise, when she reenters her profession, she will be handicapped by lack of exposure to new technologies and trends. It may be wise for her to return to work on a part-time basis in order to ease back into the profession without putting undue strain on the family.

In any relationship, there will be expectations about recreational and leisure time activities. Care should be taken early in the relationship to keep up those hobbies and recreations that are meaningful to each and also to cultivate some activities that are important to both. Money, time, and energy should be carefully budgeted so the pleasures of the recreational life do not put pressure on the vocational life or the marriage.

Having children will be part of the "hope package" brought into a marriage. As noted in an earlier chapter, the presence or absence of children in a marriage will not determine the couple's happiness. If you both want children and have them, there will be a new set of obligations placed on the relationship. This must be anticipated and planned for carefully. If you do not have children, this again should be accepted as the will of the Lord, and you can give yourself more freely to the work of the Lord and developing your Christian walk. Discussions of adoption should be delayed until much later in the relationship.

Seldom at the beginning of a marriage is the life-after-children era thought of. Plans need to be made early in married life for the child-free years following the graduation and marriage of the children. Many couples have as many years together after the family years as they did before and during the family-in-residence era. Unless the couple plans for this change, it will come as a shock to their relationship. It is amazing how many marriages fragment just as the last child is leaving home.

The temptation during the family years of the marriage is to give major attention to the children and not cultivate the marriage relationship. A couple cannot afford to do this, however, if they are to fulfill their hope of a lifelong marriage. Romance must be kept alive in the marriage during the child-rearing years, so that in the later years of life the couple will still have love in their marriage.

And, even though you don't want to think about it, it is important to plan for retirement. Studies indicate that older people seldom enjoy activities in retirement that they did not at least experiment with in their youth. Therefore, it is important to start planning at the beginning of the marriage for physical, intellectual, and social activities, hobbies, and recreations that can be continued throughout life. This means a shift from contact to spectator sports, as well as learning hobbies that do not require sharp eyes or nimble fingers.

Your Capacity to Love

Your capacity to love must continue to enlarge throughout the marriage. Ask people why they married and most will answer, "Love." Yet, they seldom knew each other long enough for love to mature. We noted earlier that love is the result of a relationship rather than the cause for one. That is why older people often look back on their years together and comment on the way love changes through the years.

In youth, love is compulsive and demanding. As the years go by, love has a way of deepening and broadening. It takes on the qualities of appreciation, gratitude, and respect. When it is expressed and cultivated, love becomes more endearing with the years.

Lois Wyse catches the developmental relationship of love in this verse (Lois Wyse, *Love Poems for the Very Married* [New York: Harper & Row Publishers, 1967], p.41):

> *Someone asked me*
> *to name the time*
> *our friendship stopped*
> *and love began.*
> *Oh, my darling,*
> *that's the secret.*
> *Our friendship*
> *never stopped.*

In a similar vein, Norman Wright observes: "Love is trusting, accepting, and believing without guarantees. It is an unconditional commitment to an imperfect person." He further describes this love as a "judgment and rational decision," not just a "strong feeling." True love for one's spouse has nothing to do with possessing him or her, but rather with affirming him or her. Norman Wright states:

> Love isn't afraid to feel; it cries out for expression. Sharing of feelings makes one more human, more real, more honest, and more lovable . . . . The richness of feelings and emotions by husband and wife adds a richness to marriage found nowhere else. (*Into the High Country* [Portland, OR: Multnomah Press, 1979], pp. 35,36.)

Hopefully you did not fall in love. Falling is an unstable condition. Rather, love is a feeling to be learned. Growing in love is more descriptive of what occurs in a Christian romantic relationship.

It is in doing things for another that love begins to grow. Edward Ford notes: "It is also through the very process of doing things with and for others that you stay in love" (Edward Ford, *Why Marriage?* [Niles, IL: Argus Communications, 1974], p. 103).

The full capacity for loving is never realized; the need for love is never filled. As a couple live together and express their love to each other, they are drawn closer and closer together. "God is love" (1 John 4:8). The more spontaneously love flows in a Christian marriage, the more like God the relationship becomes.

And, as Elizabeth Barrett Browning has observed, love never dies:

How do I love thee? Let me count the ways.
I love thee to the depth and breadth and height
My soul can reach, when feeling out of sight
For the ends of Being and ideal Grace.
I love thee to the level of everyday's
Most quiet need, by sun and candlelight.
I love thee freely, as men strive for Right;
I love thee purely, as they turn from Praise.
I love thee with the passion put to use
In my old griefs, and with my childhood's faith.
I love thee with a love I seemed to lose
With my lost saints,—I love thee with the breath,
Smiles, tears, of all my life!—and, if God choose,
I shall but love thee better after death.

The more nearly our love approximates the love of God, the more of His presence we experience in all of our relationships. It is in dating and waiting to ascertain His perfect will for our lives that total happiness can be assured.

13

Exploring Singleness

Single Is Normal

Singles come in many shapes and sizes—and ages, too. Everyone is born single. About 4 percent of the population remain single throughout their lifetime. Of the 96 percent who do marry, more than half of them can expect to become single again prematurely through death or divorce.

So, single is normal but married is usual. How we learn to handle our singleness, however, will determine the degree of fulfillment we are able to find in a marriage relationship.

Single was the original state of mankind. God created Adam as a single person. We have no idea how long Adam lived as a single, but we do know that he was 130 years old when Seth was born.

We know several other things about Adam's life as a single. He had regular communion with God, for Jehovah visited him in the cool of the evening. During his single years, Adam classified and named the animals. He had dominion over all the creatures in the Garden of Eden and cultivated the garden. God was pleased with Adam's work, according to the writer of the Book of Genesis.

How long it took Adam to develop the emotion

we call loneliness is not known. But it is evident that the first man was leading a productive life alone in the Garden for quite some time before Eve was created and introduced to him.

Loneliness was the first emotion Adam had that he could not handle alone. The order of the narrative in Genesis 2 indicates that woman was created specifically to help Adam handle the emotional need of loneliness that arose because he was a social creature living in solitude. Eve was created as a companion for fellowship and intellectual sharing. All of us, male and female, are social beings. We need each other. This is just as true of singles as it is of marrieds.

Although we are many centuries removed from Adam and Eve, it is still not good for a person to try to live totally unto himself. In the words of John Donne, "No man is an island." To reach the potential for which we were created requires social interaction, whether we are single or married.

Singles and Sexuality

The potential for sexual communication emerges at the end of the Genesis passage as a process of perpetuating human society. The result of creating woman as a mirror image of man was the potential for sexual fulfillment and procreation. Marriage does allow for meeting sexual needs, but sex was not designed to be *the* purpose for marriage. Sexual expression with a loved person of the complementary sex is a fringe benefit to total sharing which is appropriate only within the bonds of marriage.

Although marriage is a desirable goal, people

who do not marry can live happy and fulfilled lives. Sexuality is something a person is, not something he does. Single sexuality involves accepting biological maleness or femaleness and developing the appropriate gender (masculinity or femininity) that goes with sexual identification. One does not have to perform sexually to prove his sexuality!

In fact, both the Old and New Testaments are specific in giving commandments against sexual expression outside of marriage. All forms of nonmarital sex, such as fornication and adultery (both premarital and extramarital sex), incest, homosexuality, and bestiality (sex with animals), are clearly condemned in Scripture (Leviticus 18:20; Matthew 5:27; Romans 1:18-28; 1 Corinthians 5:1; 6:9,11).

Life Without Sex

How does a normal Christian single express his sexuality without sin? By affirming who he is in Christ Jesus! The term *sublimation* has been given to the process of accepting the normalcy of sexual motivation without feeling the need for sexual performance. Walt Menninger, in his book *Life Without Sex*, puts it this way:

> There is no doubt that the sexual drive is a powerful emotional force within the human personality. Yet, there are occasions when one's needs for pleasure are adequately satisfied through nonsexual activities. This is achieved through a process by which basic sexual drives are unconsciously converted into other socially acceptable endeavors. One thereby achieves substantial and lasting sources of satisfaction in life through work, play, social, and religious

121

activities. In general, the greater one's capacity to sublimate, the better one's emotional health. (Walt Menninger, *Life Without Sex* [Kansas City: Sheed Andrews and McMeel, Inc., 1976], pp. 4,5.)

The Christian single has a marvelous variety of ways to sublimate or channel his sexual impulses through work, recreation, and spiritual activities. Specifically, art, literature, music, athletics, prayer, and Bible reading (or tape listening) are marvelous ways to channel sexual energies into nonsexual activities that enrich the mind and spirit. In these activities there is no anger, guilt, or fear. No wonder Menninger suggests that the Christian single who channels sexual energies into nonsexual activities is going to enjoy better emotional health than his peers who are driven to sexual indulgence that violates divine principles.

The Christian who elects to remain single is just as normal as the Christian who elects marriage. However, the one who marries takes on added responsibilities. When God brought Adam and Eve together, He established the family as His first created institution. This was long before civil government or the church came into being. The family was and is God's primary institutional concern.

Everyone is born into a family. Everyone has the potential of contributing to the creation of a new family. But marrying and having a family is a choice, not a divine mandate. It is in dating and waiting that singles make the choice whether or not to elect marriage and family for themselves.

Jesus, Our Example

Although the Bible does not pretend to give us a

complete biography of the life of Christ, it does give us insights into His life at strategic intervals. His birth and infancy, His entrance into puberty, and His public ministry are highlighted. The writer of the Book of Hebrews assures us that Jesus "was in all points tempted like as we are, yet without sin" (Hebrews 4:15). This statement covers the entire 33½ years of His earthly life, taking Him from childhood through adolescence into adulthood.

Jesus remembers what it is like to be a child under parental authority, an adolescent with pimples, and an adult with sexual urges. Because He remembers, and is "touched with the feeling of our infirmities," He invites us to "come boldly unto the throne of grace, that we may obtain mercy, and find grace to help in time of need" (Hebrews 4:15,16).

What does He do about it? He "succors" us. "Succor" is an old Anglo-Saxon word that means to "jump and run to the assistance of." Hebrews 2:18 means that since Jesus remembers so well what it was like to be tempted in all points of single living, He will run to the assistance of His children who are being tempted by the normal problems of being single in a married society and being a Christian in a pagan culture.

Jesus does not call all Christians to a life of celibacy, but He does show us how the celibate person can lead a creative and productive life without sexual indulgence.

Single by Choice

The apostle Paul talks a great deal about being single. He implies that singleness is as much a

123

choice as marriage. Whether Paul was married and widowed young or never married is irrelevant. At the time of his missionary journeys and the writing of the Epistles, he was a single evangelist. (Acts 26:10 implies that he was a member of the Sanhedrin. Historically, marriage and a family were qualifications for membership in that august body.)

In 1 Corinthians 7:7, Paul suggests that there is a spiritual gift of singleness as well as a gift of marriage. At the time he wrote the Epistle, Paul preferred singleness for himself because of his ministerial obligations. One estate is not better than the other, Paul says, but you must accept your state, single or married, as a gift from the Lord. For some, singleness will be a lifetime commitment, but even adults who do marry must explore singleness successfully before marriage can be meaningful.

Tim Stafford has made an astute observation:

> One of the saddest things I see . . . is the tendency for single people to live life as though waiting for someone or something to happen to them. They act as though they are in limbo, waiting to become capable of life when the magic day at the altar comes. Of course, they're usually disappointed. In some cases they become such poor specimens of humanity that no one wants to marry them. More often they do get married only to discover that they haven't received the key to life; the initiative and character they should have developed before marriage is exactly what they need in marriage. And they are still lonely and frustrated. (*A Love Story* [Grand Rapids: Zondervan Publishing House, 1977], pp. 91-93.)

It is necessary to explore singleness to the full

and to become a fully functioning and happy person as a single before entering into marriage. Those who enter marriage to find happiness are destined to disappointment.

Happiness is not something we can seek and find in a relationship. Happiness follows us when we know who we are and where we are going. Happiness catches up to us when we are busy doing the Father's will and growing in Christian maturity. Jesus taught us these principles as an adolescent when He said, "I must be about my Father's business" (Luke 2:49).

You're Not Alone

According to census data, contemporary young people are remaining single longer as they delay the age of entering marriage. The median age at their first marriage in the U.S. for males is 23.5 years, which is a full year older than the average age at first marriage 20 years ago. The median age for women marrying for the first time is 21.1, again a full year older than 20 years ago. So, while the rate of marriage has not changed appreciably in recent years, there is a tendency for both males and females to remain single longer.

Unfortunately, about 40 percent of all first marriages are ending in divorce. Statistics show that there is a relationship between the age at first marriage and the incidence of divorce. The younger the couple were when they married, the higher their chances of getting divorced.

One of the contributing factors to divorce, then, is cutting short the period of singleness and entering marriage prematurely. This points out again the value of exploring singleness adequately before electing to enter marriage. Rushing into a binding relationship before one is prepared for the responsibilities as well as the privileges of marriage doesn't contribute to marital success. Many young people are not equipped to handle the pressures of a marital relationship. As a result, the average length of a first marriage is only 7 years.

Statistics further indicate that 70 percent of those whose first marriage ends in divorce marry a second time. That many of them still have not learned the lessons of life adequately is supported by the fact that 44 percent of these second marriages also end in divorce.

Dimensions of Singleness

It is imperative that Christian young people take a long, hard look at what it means to become an adult. The lessons of the teen years must be learned before the tasks of the twenties can be attacked successfully. Yes, marriage is for adults, not teenagers.

Until the dimensions of singleness have been explored adequately, it is foolhardy to seek refuge in marriage. Completeness is not found in a relationship with another human being of either sex. Completeness is found in our relationship with God and in total acceptance of ourselves as children of God (Mark 12:28-31; Romans 8:14-17).

Luke 2:52 lists four dimensions of singleness that influenced the teen and adult years of Christ. These areas must also be explored by youth today.

1. *Intellectual.* As Jesus "increased in wisdom," so each single must explore the dimensions of his intellectual capabilities. This involves

developing the mind and broadening the scope of creativity. Although the rapid growth in measured intelligence tapers off in the mid-teens, mental abilities continue to increase into the twenties and retain their efficiency until senility sets in with advanced age. At every age, the Christian, single or married, must develop mentally.

2. *Physical.* "And Jesus increased in ... stature," Luke tells us. This includes not only height and weight but all the dimensions of physical health. Jesus took good care of His body through adequate nutrition and exercise. Had He not been a vigorous man with stamina, He could never have endured the abuse that was heaped upon Him.

Throughout life, it is important to maintain good physical health routines and to keep a handle on your sexuality (James 1:27). Yes, sexual purity is still the will of God for each Christian: virginity for the never marrieds, and chastity for the marrieds.

3. *Spiritual.* As Jesus "increased ... in favor with God," so Christians of all ages must continue to develop a personal relationship with the Father. This involves both private devotions and public worship. It also includes stewardship of time, energy, and resources.

It is in worshiping and witnessing that the vitality of a personal relationship with God is demonstrated. The pattern of devotions developed as a single becomes the basis for personal and family devotions, which must prevail if a marriage is to remain Christian.

4. *Social.* Jesus, ever aware that mankind was

created a social being, "increased . . . in favor with . . . man." He never neglected being with people and demonstrated the truest marks of friendship. He communicated with individuals and groups, and was always sensitive to their needs.

Involved in our social development are career choice and civic responsibility. These choices set the atmosphere in which family life will flourish or be frustrated.

Singleness is an adventure. For some, it lasts a lifetime; for others, it is preparation for marriage and family. But, singleness as a way of life must be explored thoroughly in the teen and young adult years, before a decision about marriage is made, if full happiness in the will of God is to be enjoyed.